Youth Development in Congregations

An Exploration of the Potential and Barriers

By Eugene C. Roehlkepartain
and Peter C. Scales, Ph.D.

In collaboration with

Dale A. Blyth, Ph.D.

James J. Conway, M.Div.

Michael J. Donahue, Ph.D.

Jennifer Griffin-Wiesner

With the support of

The DeWitt Wallace–Reader's Digest Fund

This report has been made possible with the generous support
of the DeWitt Wallace–Reader's Digest Fund, New York, New York.

YOUTH DEVELOPMENT IN CONGREGATIONS: AN EXPLORATION OF THE POTENTIAL AND BARRIERS

By Eugene C. Roehlkepartain and Peter C. Scales, Ph.D.

First Printing

Search INSTITUTE
Practical research benefiting children and youth

700 South Third Street, Suite 210
Minneapolis, MN 55415
(612) 376-8955
1-800-888-7828

ISBN: 1-57482-123-7

Credits

Cover Design: Jennifer Haas

Cover Photography: Jim Whitmer/Eugene C. Roehlkepartain

Printed on recycled paper in the United States of America

CONTENTS

1. **INTRODUCTION** **7**

The Origins of this Report ■ The Nature and Scope of this Report

2. **A VISION FOR POSITIVE YOUTH DEVELOPMENT IN CONGREGATIONS** **13**

3. **UNDERSTANDING ADOLESCENTS AND THEIR NEEDS** **17**

Key Developmental Tasks in Adolescence ■ Emerging Risks ■ Societal Issues Facing Adolescents ■ Being Developmentally Responsive

4. **ASSET BUILDING: A FRAMEWORK FOR POSITIVE YOUTH DEVELOPMENT** **25**

30 Developmental Assets ■ Characteristics of an Asset-Building Approach ■ The Potential of Asset Building ■ Building Developmental Assets Through Congregations

5. **REALITIES AND POTENTIAL IN CONGREGATIONAL YOUTH PROGRAMS** **41**

Types of Religious Youth Programs ■ Leadership in Religious Youth Programs ■ Adolescents' Involvement in Congregations ■ The Impact of Religious Youth Programs ■ The Potential of Religious Youth Programs ■ Challenges to Address in Building Assets Through Congregations ■ Emerging Issues for Religious Youth Programs

6. **TRANSFORMING RELIGIOUS YOUTH WORK** **79**

Sharpening the Mission and Strategies ■ Expanding the Boundaries of Religious Youth Work ■ Engaging Youth Meaningfully ■ Rethinking Youth Worker Training and Support ■ A Challenge

7. **NOTES** **91**

LIST OF FIGURES

1.1   Background to this Project 10

4.1   External and Internal Developmental Assets that Are 27
        Important for Healthy Development

4.2   Programming Characteristics that Address 30
        the Developmental Tasks of Adolescents

4.3   The Relationship Between Developmental Assets and 37
        At-Risk Behaviors

5.1   Youth Programming Offered in Mainline Protestant Congregations . . . 44

5.2   Percent of Congregations that Regularly Offer Various 46
        Types of Programming

5.3   Training Experiences of Professional and Volunteer Youth Workers . . . 48

5.4   Youth Involvement in Congregations in Several 50
        Christian Denominations

5.5   The Relationship Between Religion and Caring Among Sixth- to 53
        Eighth-Grade Public School Students

5.6   Youth Workers' Perceptions of the Most Important Goals 56
        for their Programs

5.7   Adolescents' Ratings of their Congregations' Effectiveness in 60
        Addressing Youth Development Issues

5.8   Youth Program Goals: Gap Between Importance and Achievement 62

5.9   Religious Youth Workers' Interests in Youth Development 64
        Training and Materials

5.10   Images of the Relationship Between Youth Development and 67
        Religious/Faith Identity

5.11   Effectiveness Factors in Youth Religious Education 69

5.12   Effective Programs for Involving Hard-to-Reach Youth 72

5.13   Religious Youth Workers' Participation in Collaborative Activities . . . 74

6.1   Characteristics of Effective Asset-Building Programs 81
        in Congregations (Preliminary)

ACKNOWLEDGMENTS

We gratefully acknowledge The DeWitt Wallace–Reader's Digest Fund and Program Officer Pamela Stevens for their support of this project and this report.

PROJECT TEAM

The following people also contributed to researching, writing, editing, and producing this document: Carolyn H. Eklin, Melanie Majors, Richard J. Gordon, and Jay Petrich.

ADVISORY BOARD

The following individuals provided valuable insight into the shape of our feasibility study and to the content of this report. (Denominational and organizational affiliations are listed for identification purposes only): Ronnie Brockman *(Union of American Hebrew Congregations);* Ann Cannon *(Southern Baptist Convention);* Kenda Creasy Dean *(Princeton Theological Seminary);* Paul Fleischman *(National Network of Youth Ministries);* Bernadette Jaramillio *(Roman Catholic Church);* B.J. Long *(Congress of National Black Churches);* Karen J. Pittman *(International Youth Foundation);* Denny Rydberg *(Young Life);* Thom Schultz *(Group Publishing);* Kenneth Smith *(Chicago Theological Seminary);* Pam Stevens *(DeWitt Wallace–Reader's Digest Fund);* Branston Thurston *(United Methodist Publishing House);* Leonard Wenke *(National Federation of Catholic Youth Ministry).*

1.
INTRODUCTION

Religious youth programs have been instrumental in the development and growth of youth work in the United States. Many major national youth development organizations have religious roots (for example, YMCA and YWCA). Furthermore, religious youth programs occupy a sizable proportion of youth work in America. In Judith B. Erickson's *Directory of American Youth Organizations,* one out of three youth-serving organizations is religiously affiliated—and the listing doesn't include major denominations or the thousands of programs that occur in congregations .[1]

Despite their scope and impact on young people's lives, congregations and other religious youth programs are often forgotten or left out. With a few notable exceptions, most national reports on youth have tended to ignore the role of religious organizations in young people's lives. Major youth-serving initiatives frequently overlook religious youth programs as resources and partners.

Today, more and more observers are recognizing the importance of religious youth programs—not only for their unique role in shaping young people's spiritual development, but also for their role in nurturing the overall health and well-being of youth. Most notable among these is the landmark study by the Carnegie Council on Adolescent Development, which identifies religious youth organizations as one of five types of organizations providing community-based youth development programs. "For many adolescents," the report notes, "their religious organization and its leaders are often as trusted as family. This sense of familiarity, combined with the commitment adult church leaders have to nurture young church members, lends strength to church-based youth programs."[2]

In addition, the religious community is being recognized more and more in public life for its potential role on behalf of youth. In July 1995, President Clinton said the following in a major policy address:

Don't you believe that if every kid in every difficult neighborhood in America were in a religious institution on weekends, the synagogue on Saturday, a church on Sunday, a mosque on Friday, don't you really believe that the drug rate, the crime rate, the violence rate, the sense of self-destruction would go way down and the quality of the character of this country would go way up?[3]

THE ORIGINS OF THIS REPORT

This report grows out of a similar conviction among leaders at Search Institute and the former Center for Early Adolescence.[4] For years, both organizations have served youth workers in both secular and religious settings. Search Institute's history of research in congregations has pointed to both the potential of congregations as well as barriers to their effectiveness in youth work.

In 1995, the two organizations received a grant from the DeWitt Wallace–Reader's Digest Fund to explore the needs and interests of religious youth workers, and to explore possibilities for strengthening their ability to address the developmental need of adolescents (ages 10 to 18, with a special interest in young adolescents ages 10 to 15). (See Figure 1.1.)

KEY QUESTIONS

Several questions guided this project and serve as a backdrop to this report. They were the focus of our inquiry during the feasibility study.

- To what degree do religious youth programs see youth development as integral to their mission?

- What are the characteristics of effective youth development programming in religious contexts?

- Do religious youth workers—most of whom are volunteers—have the training and resources they need to be effective in implementing youth development programs?

- Are religious youth workers interested in becoming partners with others in their communities around youth issues?

REPORT PURPOSES

Youth Development in Congregations explores these questions and presents what we have learned through this feasibility study. It synthesizes a wide range of relevant literature and research (though research on the specific dynamics of religious youth work is sparse). In addition, it presents new findings from our study, which included a unique survey of more than 500 youth workers from multiple faith traditions.

This report has been prepared for religious youth workers, other youth workers, and leaders in youth development with the following purposes:

- To articulate the potential for religious organizations as significant contributors to efforts in positive youth development.

- To stimulate dialogue among youth workers in multiple sectors and faith traditions about the role of religious organizations in youth development.

- To spell out assumptions and build a shared vision and language between the fields of positive youth development and youth work in religious settings.

- To explore the implications of the findings for congregations, networks of youth workers, and those who serve them.

OVERVIEW

To accomplish these goals, this report does the following:

- Introduces the positive youth development framework and the realities facing adolescents, especially young adolescents.

- Summarizes the current state of knowledge and practice in religious organizations related to positive youth development.

- Explores the potential for enhancing the positive youth development aspects of youth work in religious organizations.

- Identifies the characteristics of effective youth development programming in a religious context.

THE NATURE AND SCOPE OF THIS REPORT

This report seeks to lay a conceptual foundation for the role of positive youth development in congregations and other religious youth programs. It draws from several disciplines and integrates information from several places. It is important at the outset to outline the scope of the report—and what we are not trying to do here.

YOUTH DEVELOPMENT

The focus of this report is on the role of religious youth programs in promoting positive youth development—an approach to youth work that provides supportive relationships, environments, and opportunities to nurture growth-enhancing values, skills, and commitments in adolescents.

We do not examine the role of religious youth programs in their unique task of religious or spiritual development per se. We recognize and affirm the importance of that dimension of youth work within congregations, and Search Institute has an extensive history in research on young people's spiritual development or faith formation as well.[5] In contrast, this report

FIGURE 1.1   **BACKGROUND TO THIS PROJECT**

With the support of the DeWitt Wallace–Reader's Digest Fund, Search Institute and the Center for Early Adolescence undertook an exploratory project to assess the feasibility of developing non-sectarian, geographically based, interfaith training and resources to equip religious youth leaders to enhance or develop programs with an emphasis on positive youth development for adolescents (ages 10-18, with a special interest in young adolescents ages 10-15). The project had several components.

PILOT SITES

Seven geographic sites were selected in three regions to provide a diverse base for this project. The sites included four within the major metropolitan areas of Minneapolis, St. Paul, and St. Louis, and three within medium-sized communities and rural areas in Minnesota and North Carolina. The sites were both ethnically and religiously diverse.

DISCOVERY STRATEGIES

In each of the pilot sites, the following strategies were undertaken. Together, the findings offer a comprehensive picture of issues, needs, strategies, and possibilities.

1. Youth worker interviews and focus groups—Within each site, interviews with youth workers in congregations and secular youth-serving organizations were conducted, and a focus group of congregational youth workers was convened. We discussed the needs of religious youth workers and how those needs could be met. A total of 70 youth workers were interviewed, and 44 religious youth workers participated in focus groups.

2. Census of religious youth programs—The project sought to locate every religious youth program within each of the seven sites and obtain basic information on staffing as well as the nature of programs. A total of 1,660 religious organizations were identified that might offer youth programs, and about 450 eventually completed a census form that provided a richer understanding of the youth workers and programs in these settings.

3. Survey of youth workers—A survey was conducted in the seven sites to examine needs and attitudes that might affect different training and technical assistance options. A total of 527 professional and volunteer religious youth workers completed the survey.

4. Review of existing training materials—The project sought to identify and review a wide variety of materials and training that is available around the theme of positive youth development both within and outside of a religious setting. This review of training and materials from 34 national religious and secular organizations laid the foundation for a training design that will be at the center of a later technical assistance effort.

IMPLEMENTATION PLANS

In addition to this report, we will be following up this feasibility study with a project—supported by the DeWitt Wallace–Reader's Digest Fund—to train religious youth workers in positive youth development, using Search Institute's "developmental assets" framework.

The project will involve developing networks of youth workers in local communities, then working with the networks to offer training and resources on asset building to use in congregations, and opportunities for cross-faith, community-wide activities.

explores the congregation's role in other areas of development, including the social, intellectual, emotional, social, and physical dimensions.

AGE RANGE

For the purposes of this report and project, we have chosen the ages 10 to 18 as the focus, with a special interest in young adolescents ages 10-15 (about grades 5-9). Early adolescence is a time of great physical, social, emotional, and cognitive changes that set apart that period from childhood and later adolescence. Where appropriate, we note findings or implications that relate to the different developmental periods of early and later adolescence.

CONGREGATION FOCUS

Throughout this report, we have focused attention primarily on congregations (churches, synagogues, temples, etc.) and their youth programs. We recognize that other religious youth programs effectively serve youth in many communities. However, congregational youth programs remain the most widespread, and thus the programs with the most potential impact.

LANGUAGE USAGE

Of necessity and by design, this report bridges multiple perspectives and disciplines. It seeks to build or strengthen bridges between the religious community and the more general youth development sphere (schools, community-based youth organizations, etc.). Furthermore, it seeks to build bridges across faith traditions within communities and across the country. Both of these efforts lead to challenges in selecting language that is comfortable to and appropriate for many perspectives.

• **Youth Development**—A key question we had was how much religious organizations needed to know the language and framework of positive youth development in order to be effective in building strengths in adolescents and responding to their developmental issues and needs. This report includes some terms that may not be familiar to some religious youth workers. However, our interviews, focus groups, and survey responses suggested these terms connect well with the experiences and perspectives of leaders in various faith communities.

• **Religious Diversity**—Because all faiths can and do play roles in positive youth development, we have sought to use language that is acceptable in as many traditions as possible, particularly those within the multiple Judeo-Christian traditions (Catholicism, Mainline Protestantism, Evangelicalism, Judaism), which include the vast majority of religious adherents in the United States.

THE RESEARCH BASE   A disproportionate amount of the research in this report is based on studies in a single, though broad, faith tradition: Mainline Protestantism. This lack of balance, though regrettable, reflects the general lack of quality research about youth across the wider spectrum of faith traditions. As Kenda Creasy Dean notes in a major report on religious youth work, "Research expressly devoted to religious institutions and youth is scarce, and studies concerning religious-affiliated programs for youth are even more so."[6]

Our 1995 survey, *The Attitudes and Needs of Religious Youth Workers: Perspectives from the Field* considerably broadens this research base, and these findings are included throughout this report.[7] The survey respondents included significant proportions of Catholic, Evangelical, and Fundamentalist Christian youth workers. Despite efforts to broaden the response even further, few Jewish youth workers responded. Nevertheless, this survey represents a large sample with much more diversity within Christian traditions than has previously been reported.

2.
A VISION FOR POSITIVE YOUTH DEVELOPMENT IN CONGREGATIONS

Imagine that it is the year 2001. For five years, religious youth workers from many faith traditions have been involved in intensive training around youth development issues in their community, and congregations have been implementing new strategies. Youth workers have responded eagerly to the new understanding, and programs are being reshaped to respond to adolescents' needs. Religious youth work is in the midst of a significant transformation to build "developmental assets" that provide a foundation for young people's positive development.

Visitors come from another state to see what is happening. What do they see in OurTown?

YOUTH INVOLVEMENT

The first thing the visitors notice is congregations and other religious youth organizations have become hubs of activity for youth in the community. Congregations are viewed by youth from all backgrounds and heritages as safe places where they are valued and supported, and where they can participate in challenging and exciting activities that help them develop positive values, interests, and skills.

Key to this involvement is that congregations have become inviting and welcoming places to which all the community's youth feel drawn. Young people who formerly were inactive now more regularly avail themselves of the many opportunities congregations present, and there has even been an increase in participation by youth who weren't connected formally to any congregation.

Particularly noteworthy is that youth are recognized as resources for their program as well as to the congregations and community as a whole. They have many opportunities to make a positive impact upon their wider community, and they are encouraged to develop a critical eye for viewing the community and their congregation—and a creative spirit for becoming active in improving them.

In addition, several times a year, congregations sponsor activities jointly with other local congregations of many faiths. Instead of competing to reach the core of active youth, the youth programs share a mutual goal to ensure that all youth in the community are connected to programs that best meet their needs and values.

EFFECTIVE YOUTH WORKERS

The second thing the visitors notice is that both volunteer and professional youth leaders understand adolescent needs, and the leaders have a clear sense of their congregations' roles in enhancing the healthy development of youth. Regular training and programming materials are available to equip new volunteers and leaders for their work, and to enhance and renew the skills and energy of long-time youth workers.

CONGREGATION-WIDE COMMITMENT

Caring for young people has become a major priority for OurTown's congregations. In addition to strength in the specific leadership for the youth program, most members of the congregations—not just parents and young adults—feel a responsibility for and connection to young people in an intergenerational community. In addition, parents and other family members feel involved and valued as participants in youth programs, and see the congregation as a resource in their parenting role.

RESPONSIVE PROGRAMS

One of the effects of having well-trained youth workers and congregations committed to youth is that the congregations embody characteristics that directly and indirectly enhance young people's spiritual, intellectual, emotional, social, and physical development. Programs have clear goals related to asset building that permeate all components of a congregation's work with youth—the youth program, the larger congregation, and efforts in the community.

SUPPORTIVE NETWORKS

Finally, the visitors see youth workers from throughout the community working together in a network for idea-swapping, resource-sharing, and mutual support. Joint training activities are planned and led among congregations and across sectors. Some of the veteran network members have been trained to provide ongoing training to their peers.

Religious youth workers play leadership roles in community-wide coalitions for youth. Secular and religious organizations see each other as allies and collaborate regularly to offer programs and services for youth.

CHANGED YOUTH

Most important, OurTown has seen significant changes in its young people. More of them are thriving. Fewer of them are engaged in risky behaviors. OurTown's youth are healthier, in large measure because the religious community has mobilized itself—and connected with others—to build assets that truly make a difference in the lives of young people.

This vision has many components, some of which are already integral to many congregations and some that represent the cutting edges of religious youth work. In some senses the vision grows out of the intersection of three themes:

- the developmental needs of adolescents;

- the emerging focus in youth work (both secular and religious) on positive youth development, particularly using the framework of Search Institute's "developmental assets"; and

- the characteristics and potential of religious congregations.

This report examines each of these themes, then integrates them into a new framework of characteristics of effective religious youth programs. The report concludes with key implications for religious youth workers, congregations, and those who serve them.

3.
UNDERSTANDING ADOLESCENTS AND THEIR NEEDS

Until the mid- to late-1800s, adolescence was little recognized as a separate stage of life. Only with changes such as the Industrial Revolution, the beginnings of age-grouping in schools, and the birth of pediatrics did the notion begin to take hold that there might be a distinct developmental stage between childhood and adulthood.

Psychologist G. Stanley Hall—who wrote extensively about adolescence at the turn of the century—is credited for being the "father" of adolescence as a concept. While his work was pivotal in defining the age group, he also created what we now know is an inaccurate image of adolescents. To Hall, adolescents were altogether unattractive creatures caught in ongoing "storm and stress" patterns. Thus, the period soon became thought of as something to survive.[8]

In contrast, we know today that adolescence is no more "stormy" than other periods of life, no more pathological. Furthermore, adolescents have many strengths and assets that can contribute positively to their families, schools, and communities.

A TIME OF CHANGE

While adolescence is not a time of storm and stress, it is a time of considerable change. During this time period, young people face new opportunities and challenges that play a key role in shaping their lives and futures. Change defines the lives of these young people. Among the many changes adolescents face are . . .

- The onset of puberty and its accompanying physical maturation;

- Moving from a protective neighborhood elementary school to a more distant middle-grade school;

- Traveling farther away from home without parental supervision;

- Forming new friendships and experiencing a new sense of independence from parents;

- Developing new intellectual capacities and skills; and

- Making decisions about values, vocation, education, and lifestyle.

Many of these changes revolve around several key tasks that all adolescents must accomplish as they move from childhood to adulthood. Those tasks get accomplished somewhat differently during early adolescence than in later adolescence, but the underlying issues are much the same. All adolescents must:

- develop an identity;
- come to terms with their sexuality;
- develop autonomy or independence; and
- develop a plan for their future.

Guiding adolescents through these developmental tasks becomes a key role for people who work with youth. And while it is simple to outline these tasks, real-life is more complicated. Adolescent development is multi-dimensional, inter-related, and variable. Physical, emotional, social, intellectual, and spiritual development all change, often simultaneously and sometimes dramatically. Change in one area often affects changes in another. No two adolescents of the same chronological age develop on the same schedule, and the adolescent who appears withdrawn and unfriendly at one moment can be outgoing and cheerful the next.

Addressing these changes may be particularly important during early adolescence, a time when many of the seeds of success or failure are sown. As the Carnegie Council on Adolescent Development writes in its major report, *A Matter of Time: Risk and Opportunity in the Nonschool Hours*: "With the exception of infancy, no time in life compresses more physical, intellectual, social, emotional, or moral development into so brief a span [as early adolescence]."[9]

The developmental tasks of adolescence prompt all adolescents to ask themselves three basic questions, to which they need affirmative answers:

- Am I competent?
- Am I normal?
- Am I lovable and loving?[10]

As they seek answers to these questions, adolescents, especially young adolescents, explore and question. These activities are normal aspects of development that occur in adolescents' spiritual journeys as well.[11] Because of their increasing cognitive capcity, young adolescents begin to think critically about the values they hold—and the values held by parents and other significant adults in their lives. Older adolescents reach tentative conclusions about either accepting or rejecting these teachings.

Because of their emerging thinking skills, young adolescents can begin to grapple with great moral, ethical, theological, and spiritual themes such as justice, compassion, faith, prayer, and creation. They can begin to think of scripture in new ways and to reflect on its importance to them.

At the same time, these inquisitive young adolescents may begin to question deeply valued tenets of their faith tradition as they move into a stage that John H. Westerhoff III describes as "searching faith" in his influential work. This stage, he writes, is "characterized by questioning, critical judgment, and experimentation."[12]

EMERGING RISKS

Not only are adolescents laying the foundation for their success in life, they are also in a time when they are making critical decisions about potentially dangerous behaviors, including alcohol and other drug use, sexual experience, and gang involvement.

About 80 percent of young adolescents negotiate the period smoothly or with just minor difficulties. However, their adult-like physical development, greater freedom from continual parental scrutiny, the desire to explore new experiences, and relatively immature decision-making skills combine to produce a riskier climate than experienced during childhood.

Surveys of 250,000 sixth- to 12th-grade public school students by Search Institute have examined the prevalence of risky behaviors. One-third of sixth-graders display two or more of the 20 at-risk behaviors identified. This involvement increases to 54 percent by ninth grade and 74 percent by 12th grade.[13] Specific behaviors illustrate the pattern:

Percent at risk for . . .[14]	Sixth grade	Ninth grade	12th grade
Binge drinking	9%	21%	39%
Sexual intercourse	7%	24%	59%
Vandalism	5%	11%	19%

Thus, at a time when adolescents are shaping their lifestyles, beliefs, values, and futures, too many—particularly those living in poverty[15]—are setting off on trajectories shaped by regrettable choices with far-reaching, long-term consequences.

MISMATCHED PROGRAMS Despite the critical issues that emerge during early adolescence, the nation's understanding of this age group remains inadequate, filled with misperceptions of the characteristics, developmental needs, and strengths of these young people. For example, while most schools serving young adolescents now operate with the developmentally responsive structure of middle schools (grades 6-8), special teacher training remains uncommon, and only one-third to one-half of "middle schools" are developmentally responsive in more than name alone.[16]

A similar, if not greater, lag in understanding appears to be present in the religious community. Most existing resources and approaches to youth work in Protestant Christian traditions have adopted a "junior high ministry" model (grades 7-9), which schools are abandoning.[17]

One encouraging sign is that more high schools have begun to operate like good middle schools, especially in trying to give students more personalized attention and connections to adults. This shows recognition that the needs of all adolescents are similar in kind, although different in degree at different developmental stages.

Early adolescence is a crucial period for congregations because an opportunity missed to make connections between young adolescents and congregational life is not easily recaptured during the senior high years. It is also a time when many faith traditions have intensive religious instruction and rites of passage (e.g. confirmation and bar/bat mitzvah). Therefore, it makes sense to have a special understanding of what middle-schoolers need and how that contrasts with what senior high youth need.

At the same time, there is danger in abandoning older youth in congregations. Because of increased competition for young people's time, many congregations do little to offer opportunities for older youth. As a result, they become even less connected to the religious communities that can offer guidance and support as they move into adulthood.

SOCIETAL ISSUES FACING ADOLESCENTS

These developmental themes intersect with a series of issues in society and American culture that heighten the need to pay more attention to the positive development of youth. These issues include the following:

UNSTRUCTURED TIME In 1992, the Carnegie Council on Adolescent Development drew national attention to the fact that about 40 percent of young adolescents' waking hours are discretionary. Some communities provide many opportunities for young adolescents to spend their free time in constructive, stimulating activities. In other cases, however, the free time provides opportunities for experimenting with and developing negative behaviors. The risks are particularly pronounced for young people in high-risk neighborhoods that are unsafe and have few constructive opportunities for youth.[18]

Older adolescents have even more freedom to fill their time as they choose, and some different options. They are more likely to drive, more likely to have a part-time job, and more likely to engage in nearly all risky behaviors than are younger adolescents. Among 10th graders, just 25 percent of the time they spend out of school is involved in productive pursuits such as homework, reading, or supervised extracurricular activities.[19]

NEGATIVE PERCEPTIONS

At a time when youth need affirmation and support, they instead encounter hesitation and fear. Because of widespread misunderstandings of adolescent development as a stormy, difficult period, adolescents must deal with negative attitudes and perceptions about them.

Polls of youth in Chicago and Minnesota have found that most young adolescents think adults have negative attitudes about them, and that their perceptions of these negative attitudes remain stable throughout older adolescence.[20] Laurence Steinberg and Ann Levine summarize the perceptions in our culture this way:

> *The idea that adolescence equals trouble has been part of our folklore, handed down from generation to generation, and accepted by psychologists, educators, and parents alike. . . . Parents who haven't run into serious problems, who actually enjoy their teenagers, end up being apologetic: "I guess we're just lucky." It's not luck.[21]*

During a time when adolescents are struggling with questions of identity and self-worth, it is difficult, if not impossible, not to take these perceptions personally.

LACK OF CONNECTIONS

Perhaps as an outgrowth, in part, of the negative images of adolescents, many lack positive connections to individuals and institutions that can nourish, support, and value them. For some, not even their families provide this nurture, and other adults in communities often do not see it as their responsibility. As Joan Wynn and her colleagues conclude, we are faced with a society-wide "depletion of adult resources for youth."[22]

A study by the National Commission on Children asks 10- to 17-year-old youth to name "special adults who really care about them"; many mention their mother (94 percent) and father (82 percent), but only a minority of youth mention other adults (particularly outside the extended family):

- Grandparent (43 percent)
- Aunt, uncle, cousin, or other relative (41 percent)
- Teacher or coach (33 percent)
- Adult friend or neighbor (16 percent)
- Leader of a youth group, priest, rabbi, or minister (15 percent)[23]

Furthermore, many young people are not connected to supportive institutions. For example, only 30 percent of 6th- to 12th-grade students surveyed in *The Troubled Journey* experience a caring and encouraging school climate.[24] And in its study of mainline Protestant congregations, Search Institute discovered that 47 percent of church-going 13- to 15-year-old youth rarely or never experience caring adults in the congregation.[25]

GROWING UP TOO FAST

In the 1980s, David Elkind's books *The Hurried Child* and *All Grown Up and No Place to Go* identified the pervasive pressures children face through adolescence to be "little adults."[26] Whether it's pressure to succeed in school, dress like adults, absorb adult-oriented media, or cope with adult problems, it has become very difficult to provide a childhood in which a young person has the time to sort out critical issues of identity and development. "Growth into personhood in our contemporary society takes time and cannot be hurried," Elkind writes. "When children are pressured to grow up too fast, important achievements are skipped or bypassed, which can give rise to serious problems later."[27]

A corollary to the theme of growing up too fast is the lack of many significant markers or rites of passage in this culture. As traditional rites have lost their influence and significance for many families, little is left to mark—and celebrate—important transitions. As Elkind writes, "Markers protect teenagers against stress by helping them attain a clear self-definition, and they reduce stress by supplying rules, limits, taboos, and prohibitions that liberate teenagers from the need to make age-inappropriate decisions and choices."[28]

GENDER AND RACE

Though gender and race are clearly issues of personal identity, they are also important societal issues at this particular time in history. Several social phenomena suggest that these issues have a serious impact:

- Despite gains in women's rights and issues of gender equity, young girls continue to face obstacles in education.[29]

- Girls appear to be more vulnerable in early adolescence than boys, partly because their development is accelerated compared to boys.

Furthermore, girls who mature early may face additional pressure or discrimination from adults.[30]

- Shifting demographics among young people will increasingly impact young adolescent programming in the United States. Current trends suggest that the percent of young adolescents of color will continue to grow so that, by 2000, 34 percent of adolescents will be people of color.[31] In several major urban areas (including New York and Los Angeles), white people already have become a minority.

- Young people increasingly are the victims as well as the perpetrators of crimes, with young black men disproportionately likely to lead in these statistics.[32]

These issues—though relevant throughout society—have a particular impact on adolescents because they are developing their sense of personal identity, their values, and their world views.

BEING DEVELOPMENTALLY RESPONSIVE

Earlier we noted that adolescents are asking themselves three basic questions: Am I competent? Am I normal? Am I lovable and loving? A key responsibility of people and programs that touch the lives of young people is to ensure that all youth—regardless of the social pressures they face—say "yes" to these questions.[33]

The challenge is not only to understand the complexity of how adolescents develop, but then to develop programs and opportunities that respond to those realities, needs, and strengths. Too often, schools, congregations, and other youth programs simply repackage what they used to do or what they do for other age groups and apply that understanding to young adolescents. In addition, programs don't tap sufficiently into older adolescents' need for increased opportunities to develop career interests or make more sophisticated decisions. What's needed is an approach that begins with an understanding of the developmental issues and builds programs in direct response to these issues.

4.
ASSET BUILDING: A FRAMEWORK FOR POSITIVE YOUTH DEVELOPMENT

A growing body of research is convincing youth workers and other youth experts that youth work in all settings must shift its focus. Since at least the 1960s, a disproportionate amount of youth programming has operated out of an intervention model of only addressing problems after they are widespread. Communities, families, and institutions have identified things they do not want youth to do, then have responded accordingly. As Karen J. Pittman often says, "Problem-free does not mean fully prepared."[34]

Perhaps as a result of a focus on preventing problems, organizations have neglected to provide the support, boundaries, opportunities, competencies, values, and commitments that provide the foundation upon which young people build healthy lives and promising futures. Without these building blocks of development, young people do not have the resources that guide them to healthy choices. Ironically, the best way to prevent youth problems may be to focus, not on preventing them, but on promoting assets that respond to what young people need developmentally.

DEFINITION

In response to the developmental needs outlined in Chapter 3, a new approach has emerged in youth work called "positive youth development."

> *Positive youth development is an approach to youth work that focuses on providing supportive relationships, environments, and opportunities to nurture in adolescents growth-enhancing values, skills, and commitments.*[35]

Whereas much youth work has focused on identifying and addressing problems, positive youth development takes another approach. Instead of beginning with the problems, it begins by asking what young people need to navigate successfully through adolescence.

30 DEVELOPMENTAL ASSETS

To begin answering this question, Search Institute examined the research from a number of fields, including resiliency, prevention, developmental psychology, social psychology, and sociology to name factors in young people's lives that are important for their healthy development. A total of 30 assets were identified that provide a developmental foundation for youth. They involve surrounding young people with consistent systems of support, boundaries, and structure (external assets) and nurturing in them the commitments, values, and competencies (internal assets) that help them thrive and make wise choices.

Sixteen external assets and 14 internal assets have been identified and measured by Search Institute (Figure 4.1).

EXTERNAL ASSETS

Adolescents are influenced—both positively and negatively—by individuals, institutions, and social norms around them. The goal of positive youth development is to surround young people with "external assets" that will be positive influences. Peter L. Benson summarizes the perspective this way:

> *Positive development requires constant exposure to interlocking systems of support, control, and structure. In the ideal, young people— through schools, families, community organizations, and religious institutions—constantly interact with caring, principled adults. These patterns serve as external assets, providing young people with webs of safety and love important for stimulating and nurturing healthy development.*[36]

The external assets are divided into three broad categories:

- **Support**—Young people need families, other people, and places that are caring, supportive, affirming, and safe.

- **Boundaries**—Young people need standards and rules to guild them.

- **Structured time use**—Young people need positive, interesting, and challenging things to do with their time.

INTERNAL ASSETS

One goal of surrounding youth with external assets is to nurture in them internal assets—attitudes, commitments, values, and competencies that help them make wise choices. "Strength in internal assets creates a centeredness among youth that promotes wise, health-enhancing choices and minimizes risk taking," Benson writes.[37] These internal assets can be divided into three categories:

- **Educational commitment**—Young people need to develop personal commitments to learning and education.

FIGURE 4.1

EXTERNAL AND INTERNAL DEVELOPMENTAL ASSETS THAT ARE IMPORTANT FOR HEALTHY DEVELOPMENT[38]

EXTERNAL ASSETS	
ASSET TYPE	**ASSET NAME AND DEFINITION**
Support	1. **Family support**—Family life provides high levels of love and support.
	2. **Parent(s) as social resources**—Youth views parent(s) as accessible resources for advice and support.
	3. **Parent communication**—Youth has frequent, in-depth conversations with parent(s).
	4. **Other adult resources**—Youth has access to non-parent adults for advice and support.
	5. **Other adult communication**—Youth has frequent, in-depth conversations with non-parent adults.
	6. **Parent involvement in schooling**—Parent(s) are involved in helping youth succeed in school.
	7. **Positive school climate**—School provides a caring, encouraging environment.
Boundaries	8. **Parental standards**—Parent(s) have standards for appropriate conduct.
	9. **Parental discipline**—Parent(s) discipline student when a rule is violated.
	10. **Parental monitoring**—Parent(s) monitor "where I am going and with whom I will be."
	11. **Time at home**—Youth goes out for "fun and recreation" three or fewer nights per week.
	12. **Positive peer influence**—Youth's best friends model responsible behavior.
Structured Time Use	13. **Involved in music**—Youth spends three hours or more per week in music training or practice.
	14. **Involved in school extra-curricular activities**—Youth spends one hour or more per week in school sports, clubs, or organizations.
	15. **Involved in community organizations or activities**—Youth spends one hour or more per week in organizations or clubs outside of school.
	16. **Involved in a church or synagogue**—Youth spends one hour or more per week attending programs or services.

FIGURE 4.1 (CONTINUED)

INTERNAL ASSETS	
ASSET TYPE	**ASSET NAME AND DEFINITION**
Educational Commitment	17. **Achievement motivation**—Youth is motivated to do well in school. 18. **Educational aspiration**—Youth aspires to pursue post-high school education (e.g., trade school, college). 19. **School performance**—Youth reports that her or his school performance is above average. 20. **Homework**—Youth reports doing six hours or more of homework per week.
Positive Values	21. **Values helping people**—Youth places high personal value on helping other people. 22. **Is concerned about world hunger**—Youth reports interest in helping to reduce world hunger. 23. **Cares about people's feelings**—Youth cares about other people's feelings. 24. **Values sexual restraint**—Youth values postponing sexual intercourse.
Social Competence	25. **Assertiveness skills**—Youth can stand up for what he or she believes. 26. **Decision-making skills**—Youth is good at making decisions. 27. **Friendship-making skills**—Youth is good at making friends. 28. **Planning skills**—Youth is good at planning ahead. 29. **Self-esteem**—Youth has high self-esteem. 30. **Positive view of personal future**—Youth is optimistic about her or his personal future.

- **Positive values**—Young people need a core of positive beliefs and convictions that guide their priorities and behaviors.

- **Social competencies**—Young people need to develop skills and abilities that help them function as independent, competent people.[39]

While other assets could be added,[40] this list provides a beginning point for thinking of the types of positive influences that are important for youth. They also point toward some of the characteristics of an asset-building or positive youth development approach.

CHARACTERISTICS OF AN ASSET-BUILDING APPROACH

The framework of assets provides a focus for understanding the dimensions of positive youth development. Several principles and characteristics undergird the approach.

DEVELOPMENTALLY RESPONSIVE

Positive youth development—and asset building in particular—begins with an understanding of young people's characteristics, needs, strengths, and challenges, then responds to these appropriately. Strategies are adjusted to respond to what the young people are like, rather than expecting the young people to adjust to the program because "we've always done it this way" or because it works for older or younger youth or youth in another setting or situation.

Being developmentally responsive also means developing programs that interest and engage adolescents. A report on "resiliency" from the National Assembly of National Voluntary Health and Social Welfare Organizations identified the following characteristics of programs that respond to the developmental level of the youth involved. (Also see Figure 4.2) Effective programs . . .

- Offer a diverse array of activities that attract and engage young people;

- Are age-appropriate and age-sensitive, providing extra support during key transition times;

- Are centered in places young people can get to; and

- Make sure all youth can afford to participate.[41]

FIGURE 4.2

PROGRAMMING CHARACTERISTICS THAT ADDRESS THE DEVELOPMENTAL TASKS OF ADOLESCENTS

	TYPICAL DEVELOPMENTAL TASKS	RESPONSIVE PROGRAMMING CHARACTERISTICS
EMOTIONAL	• Develop a sense of personal identity • Nourish personal autonomy and control • Develop self-competencies such as coping, decision-making, and stress management • Continue development of self-esteem	• Respect individual differences in youth • Provide opportunities for youth to develop decision-making and other self-competencies • Provide an affirming, caring climate
INTELLECTUAL	• Integrate new capacity for abstract thinking • Increase knowledge • Build critical thinking skills • Experience competence through academic achievement • Learn from doing	• Provide a climate that nurtures thinking skills and allows youth to ask questions • Challenge youth with new knowledge • Youth are given opportunities to express their creativity
PHYSICAL	• Understand the changes that occur in puberty and begin maturing physically • Improve movement skills through physical activity • Form healthy habits that promote lifelong fitness • Learn to take and manage appropriate physical risks	• Engage all youth in physical activity • Provide opportunities for physical challenges and appropriate risks • Address health-related issues (sexuality, alcohol and other drugs, diet and nutrition, and others)
SOCIAL	• Improve communication skills • Deepen abilities to form meaningful relationships with peers and adults • Explore adults' rights and responsibilities	• Give safe opportunities for youth to talk together about serious topics • Work in small groups that provide intimacy with adults and youth • Give youth leadership and ownership in the program
SPIRITUAL/ MORAL	• Develop personal values • Enhance a sense of responsibility and accountability to the world • Apply values and beliefs to personal actions	• Encourage youth to articulate their own values • Challenge youth to express concern through service and justice-related activities • Connect personal/spiritual values to choices in life

A POSITIVE VISION

In the previous chapter, we noted that adolescence has long been perceived in negative terms. Yet more than 20 years of research confirms that, for the majority of youth and families, adolescence is a positive experience. In reacting to the common negative perceptions, Steinberg and Levine write:

> *Adolescence is not an inherently difficult period. Psychological problems, problem behavior, and family conflict are no more common in adolescence than in any other stage of the life cycle. . . . The problems we have come to see as a "normal" part of adolescent development . . . are not normal at all. They are both preventable and treatable. The bottom line is that good kids don't suddenly go bad in adolescence.*[42]

Asset building does not focus on preventing problems (what youth should not do). Rather, it focuses on recognizing and building strengths and assets that enable young people to make positive choices in all areas of their lives.

YOUTH LEADERSHIP

In contrast to the common negative perceptions of adolescents, asset building is guided by a positive vision of youth, their needs, and their role in the world. It seeks to identify and build on the strengths that adolescents have. It sees them as resources to their families, their schools, their communities, their congregations—not as problems to avoid or fix. This perspective gives consistency, direction, and energy to efforts that involve and benefit youth.

Part of recognizing young adolescents as resources is involving them in leadership in the programs that affect them. "One reason youth involvement works," asserts the report from the National Assembly, "is because it creates a sense of ownership on the part of the young. Programs they are directly involved in are no longer something adults do for them, they are their programs which they do with adults."[43]

AWARENESS OF THE WHOLE PERSON

In a positive youth development approach, the young person is seen as a whole, and programming seeks to address the multiple dimensions of life. In other words, the approach recognizes that the physical needs are not isolated from the emotional, spiritual, or intellectual needs; each influences the others. (This is true, of course, of all ages, not just adolescence.)

Yet most of the programs and services for children and youth have become so specialized that they neglect the interconnections. One observer described the current situation like this:

In looking at a high-risk teenager, an educator sees a student in danger of dropping out, a health care provider sees a patient at risk of having a low birthweight baby, a social worker sees a client who may need public assistance, and a religious leader may see the troubled offspring of a personal friend. Who sees the whole young adolescent?[44]

It is nonsensical to expect only families to handle emotional needs, only schools to handle intellectual needs, only friends to handle social needs, and only congregations to handle spiritual or moral needs. Young people do not live in such a splintered fashion. Rather, each institution or individual influences all aspects of a young person, and that influence needs to become intentional to have a positive, thoughtful impact.

COOPERATION AMONG SOCIALIZING SYSTEMS

Because positive youth development views adolescents as whole persons, it also places them in the context of family, school, community, and the world. It calls for a new way of doing business. Schools, family support programs, congregations, youth-serving organizations, public services, and others must not only all work with youth, but with each other.

Positive youth development recognizes that adolescent behavior is shaped by expectations and relationships, and that adolescents must perceive consistent expectations and caring relationships across the multiple dimensions of their lives. People and institutions who shape young people's lives cannot provide this consistency unless they work together across organizational and disciplinary boundaries.

In addition to cooperation among the institutions that serve youth is a critical need for a new sense of shared responsibility with families. Too often, people point to the family as the source of problems, yet little is done to support families. On the other hand, families too often turn over their children to schools or congregations or others, expecting those programs to provide young people with whatever they need in a particular area, such as spiritual development or education.

There is a critical need for everyone to contribute and for families to partner with schools, congregations, community-based organizations, and others to provide young people with the support, boundaries, and structure that they need to thrive.

RELATIONAL FOCUS

Nurturing assets cannot be done by programs alone. At the heart of a positive youth development approach is healthy, caring relationships for adolescents—with peers, with parents, and with other adults. "All youth need at least one ongoing, caring relationship with an adult," the National Assembly asserts. "It can be a parent, mentor, coach, teacher, neighbor, or volunteer. Successful programs plan to create these relationships."[45]

The goal is not to create programs or hire professionals to substitute for caring relationships. Rather, the goal is to enhance all of young people's relationships, and to build new relationships of support, caring, and guidance. Benson puts it this way:

> *Asset building has less to do with hiring more "experts" than it does with activating the capacity of people in a community to build both formal and informal relationships with young people. . . . Every young person ought to have sustained relationships with dozens of adults of all ages, in neighborhoods, religious institutions, teams, businesses, places of employment, and schools.*[46]

ALL YOUTH

Much of the programming for youth in the past 20 years has focused on particular populations. Young people have been given labels (at-risk , gifted, challenged, etc.), then highly focused programs have been designed to address those specific issues. While the goals of these approaches have been laudable, they have had some unanticipated negative effects.

- First, young people have been labeled, and that label has branded them and boxed them into narrow places in society. They have become known more by their labels (which are typically viewed in negative terms) than their total personhood.

- Second, programs for youth have become fragmented and over-specialized. One study illustrates this problem well: "A runaway shelter will not accept teenagers who have drinking problems, a maternity home will not accept pregnant teens who are 'disturbed,' and a psychiatric clinic will not treat a youngster who is retarded or deaf."[47]

A positive youth development approach focuses on building the basic assets that *all* youth need, thus avoiding both the need for labels and the trend toward fragmentation. In surveying youth in communities across the United States, we consistently find that a vast majority of young people have far too few of these assets in their lives. Out of 250,000 sixth- to 12th-grade public school students surveyed, more than three-fourths report fewer than 20 of the 30 assets.

This perspective challenges congregations to broaden their understanding of the youth they serve and to reach out to youth that may have previously fallen beyond their programs. Writing in a preface to *A Matter of Time*, Wilma Tisch, chairman of the Board of the WNYC Foundation, expresses the issue this way:

> *A clear pattern emerged as we looked systematically at the many subsectors within the large universe of organizations and institutions*

that we had selected for analysis: Without exception, the young people in greatest need had the least access to support and services. Whether our particular focus . . . was publicly funded recreation programs, religious youth groups, sports programs, or private, nonprofit youth organizations, we found that young people in more advantaged circumstances had greater access to current programs and services.[48]

This focus also calls for programs to become more diverse—and to celebrate that diversity. According to a report from the National Assembly:

Youth development programs that work demonstrate cultural awareness, sensitivity, and competence. They not only address the issue of diversity, setting aside assumptions and stereotypes, but value differences of race, language, income level, ethnic background, and disability in their programs as strengths. Valuing diversity must be at the foundation of successful programs, not simply a nice add-on.[49]

ALL SECTORS

Finally, positive youth development recognizes that no single sector in a community does—or could—adequately provide everything young adolescents need to grow up healthy. In the past, communities have implicitly and explicitly "divided" the young person and given each sector responsibility to address one issue or another. The result, however, was that few of the individual pieces were done well because they were not done with an understanding of the whole.

This approach advocates a different perspective. All sectors have a responsibility to "the whole person." For example, no program focusing on the moral character or religious development of young people will be successful if it does not address those issues in the context of the physical, intellectual, social, and emotional issues that are also tied to moral and religious development.

Furthermore, this approach calls for all individuals and organizations that influence the lives of youth to affirm the value of each other's efforts, support those efforts, and work cooperatively toward a common vision for young people. In the process, young people will be surrounded in all areas of their lives with the assets they need to grow up healthy.[50]

Congregations may have a particularly valuable role to play in uniting communities on behalf of youth. In some communities (most notably many African American communities), congregations remain one of the strongest institutions.

In addition, the American public tends to have confidence in congregations' ability to act. A Gallup survey found that people are most likely to have confidence in congregation's ability to solve local problems. Overall, 57 percent of adults surveyed said they have a "great deal" or "quite a bit of confidence" that congregations have the ability to deal with problems facing the community—the highest of any institution. Volunteer groups and schools are next at 54 percent and 47 percent, respectively.[51]

THE POTENTIAL OF ASSET BUILDING

To this point, we have focused primarily on the theoretical rationale for positive youth development and asset building. A growing body of research supports this approach as having the potential for tremendous impact on adolescents, both in terms of increasing positive outcomes and decreasing negative outcomes. Furthermore, this approach appears to be more effective in addressing critical risks among youth—premature sexual intercourse, violence, alcohol and other drug use, school failure—than a range of prevention approaches that have been found to have little long-term impact.[52]

In addition, there is growing evidence that positive youth development can be particularly valuable for youth who are vulnerable due to poverty and other deficits—youth who represent an important outreach opportunity for congregations.

INCREASE POSITIVE OUTCOMES FOR YOUTH

Since the goal of positive youth development is to promote the healthy development of young people, it is important to know whether that actually occurs. Though the research in this area does not have a long history, the evidence is mounting to suggest that it works:

- Search Institute has found that youth who have more assets in their lives are more likely to do well in school and to exhibit caring behaviors (such as volunteering).[53]

- Research by Reginald M. Clark found that young people who spend 20 to 35 hours a week in "constructive learning activity" are more likely to be successful in school. These constructive activities might include meaningful discussions with peers and adults, leisure reading, writing, homework, hobbies, chores, and healthy games.[54]

INCREASE POSITIVE OUTCOMES FOR SOCIETY

A focus on the positive unleashes adolescents to become significant contributors to and resources for their communities. Adolescents—even those who are faced with major obstacles to their development—can become agents of positive community change when they are encouraged and empowered to contribute to others. *A Matter of Time* summarizes the potential this way: "Communities that respond to teenagers' needs can expect a remarkable gift in return: an outpouring of youthful energy, enthusiasm, and idealism that will benefit both the young people themselves and the community as a whole."[55]

The long-term potential is also important to remember. When youth develop the skills, values, and commitments they need to make positive choices as teenagers, they carry those assets with them into adulthood. We can expect more productive workers, healthier relationships, and deeper commitments if we focus during adolescence on building the foundational assets that will guide and sustain young people into adulthood.

REDUCE NEGATIVE OUTCOMES FOR YOUTH

Since 1989, Search Institute research has measured the presence of 30 assets in more than 250,000 youth in more than 450 communities across the United States. This research has shown the powerful relationship between developmental assets and at-risk behaviors. Young people who experience these assets are much less likely to become involved in a whole range of at-risk behaviors. (See Figure 4.3.)

Furthermore, this same research has found that assets are particularly important in promoting "resiliency" in youth, helping them beat the odds. Despite their experiences of physical or sexual abuse, parental addiction, and other "deficits," substantial proportions of youth avoid negative behaviors. And it appears that one key to their success is that they have more assets in their lives, counterbalancing the negative forces working against them. In short, by concentrating on building these assets in young people, we have the potential to reduce significantly many at-risk behaviors with all types of youth and in all types of communities.

REDUCE NEGATIVE OUTCOMES FOR SOCIETY

The reduction in at-risk behaviors among youth is not only good for youth, but it also has enormous positive benefit for society. Whether the focus is on adolescent pregnancy, juvenile crime, or violence, much of our national energy is consumed trying to patch up problems that are preventable—problems that are due, in part, to the fact that too many young people do not have the assets they need to make healthy choices.

No single approach or program will eliminate these problems. Too many factors influence human behavior. But the evidence is strong that rebuilding the developmental infrastructure for adolescents will go a long way toward reducing the scope of the problems so the need for extensive prevention and intervention efforts becomes the exception, not the rule, in work with adolescents.

FIGURE 4.3 — THE RELATIONSHIP BETWEEN DEVELOPMENTAL ASSETS AND AT-RISK BEHAVIORS[56]

The following table shows that sixth- to 12th-grade public school youth with more assets in their lives are much less likely to be involved in a range of problem behaviors. Furthermore, those with more assets are more likely to engage in positive behavior. Percentages indicate the youth who report each behavior, based on the number of assets they report.

PATTERNS OF HIGH-RISK BEHAVIORS*	PERCENT WHO REPORT EACH RISKY BEHAVIOR AMONG YOUTH WITH . . .				
	TOTAL	0-10 ASSETS	11-20 ASSETS	21-25 ASSETS	26-30 ASSETS
Alcohol—Six or more uses in past month or got drunk once or more in past two weeks	**22%**	44%	23%	9%	3%
Tobacco—Smokes one or more cigarettes every day or uses smokeless tobacco regularly	**16%**	35%	16%	4%	1%
Illicit drugs—Six or more uses of illicit drugs in the past year	**9%**	22%	9%	2%	1%
Sexual activity—Sexual intercourse, two or more times	**32%**	51%	34%	17%	7%
Depression/suicide—Frequently depressed and/or has attempted suicide	**23%**	42%	24%	11%	5%
Anti-social behavior/violence—Two or more acts of antisocial behavior in the past year	**28%**	51%	28%	13%	6%
School failure—Skipped school two or more days in the past month, and/or wants to drop out	**13%**	30%	12%	4%	1%
Vehicle recklessness—Drinks and drives, rides with drinking driver, or non-use of seat belts	**54%**	78%	57%	35%	19%
PROSOCIAL BEHAVIORS					
Volunteer service—Volunteers one or more hours per week	**37%**	15%	34%	57%	75%
Success in school—Gets mostly A's in school	**18%**	5%	13%	28%	51%

*Definitions are designed to show engagement in patterns of risky behavior, not just single acts of experimentation.

IMPACT ON VULNERABLE YOUTH

Given the preponderance of evidence that youth in high-risk environments—those who experience deficits such as poverty, abuse, neglect, and parental addiction—face the greatest challenges in developing a healthy, productive lifestyle, it is particularly important to consider whether, in fact, a positive youth development approach effectively enhances their opportunities for development. As Karen Pittman puts it, "Organizations in the voluntary sector should be assessed not only on their ability to 'make a good kid better' but to help those in trouble or at risk of being in trouble."[57]

While pieces of evidence are mounting to support the value of an asset-promoting approach for youth in high-risk environments, there is a clear need for more research to determine the characteristics of positive youth development programs that are particularly effective with vulnerable youth.

Though it does not include youth in major urban areas, *The Troubled Journey* does identify youth who experience a number of "deficits" that threaten healthy development. In particular, it examines youth who report being physically or sexually abused, living with an addicted parent, or living in a single-parent household. Then it compares youth in these situations who are engaged in multiple at-risk behaviors to those who are involved in few or no at-risk behaviors.

Benson discovered that major factors distinguishing the "thriving" youth from those who are not thriving is the presence or absence of the developmental assets. Thriving youth are much more likely to . . .

- hold strong educational commitments;
- hold positive values;
- be connected to adult-led, structured youth programs, including religious institutions;
- have families that set boundaries or exercise appropriate control; and
- be surrounded by adult care, concern, and support.[58]

Though this research cannot fully answer the questions related to poverty and high-risk urban areas, it does suggest that an asset-promoting strategy holds promise for youth in these communities.

We believe asset building is highly compatible with the missions of the vast majority of congregations in the United States. Healthy adolescent development is seen as a central goal across the denominational and theological spectrum and is linked to the belief that religious youth work involves addressing people's well-being at many levels. It also grows out of a desire to provide a caring community for all people, not just youth.

Many of the themes highlighted in this chapter are foundational in current understandings of religious youth work. Religious youth work has learned a great deal about adolescent development and has sought to apply those insights to programming. Indeed, in some faith traditions, religious institutions and leaders have been at the forefront of efforts to enhance the well-being of young people.

At the same time, not all congregations have a clear commitment to or vision for a comprehensive approach to youth development. They may offer a smorgasbord of programming that is fun or entertaining, but not centered in a clear sense of purpose and direction.

Thus, for some, this chapter is a call to reclaim or reaffirm their perspective and tradition in nurturing the development of the whole child. For others, it may be a challenge to build an intentional focus on youth development in programming for adolescents.

In both cases, intentional efforts to enhance religious youth programs with an emphasis on building developmental assets has tremendous impact for the good not only of youth, but also for congregations and society. The next chapter focuses on the realities and opportunities for youth development within congregations.

5.
REALITIES AND POTENTIAL IN CONGREGATIONAL YOUTH PROGRAMS

Despite their presence in every community and their potential for reaching many youth, very little is known from research about youth programs in congregations. The extent of participation by vulnerable youth and the possibility of expanding their involvement has also not yet been thoroughly assessed. However, the accumulating evidence suggests that congregations have an impressive ability and potential to touch the lives of adolescents and their families.

What is less clear, though, is whether or not the programs actually reach their potential and offer programming that has significant positive impact. This chapter explores these questions by examining the state of religious youth work and its potential for positive youth development. Our 1995 survey of religious youth workers, *The Attitudes and Needs of Religious Youth Workers,* offers much illuminating information, and we draw frequently on this new data in this chapter.[59]

TYPES OF RELIGIOUS YOUTH PROGRAMS

To set the foundation for discussion, it is important to be clear about what we mean by religious youth programs. These programs are typically part of a congregation's program. However a sizable group of para-congregation organizations (such as Young Life) also offer religious programming in communities. These groups are generally not part of a congregational youth program, though they may be sponsored by congregations. Where relevant, the dynamics of these programs are explicitly addressed. However, the majority of the information in this chapter is based on congregational youth programming.

The primary targets of most religious youth programs have been high school students, grades nine to 12. However, recent years have seen a decline in participation among this age group, and an increase in participation (and programming interest in) youth in grades six to eight, a time when young people are more likely to be involved in formal religious education (e.g. Sunday or Sabbath school as well as confirmation or bar/bat mitzvah). Furthermore, research indicates great difficulty in gaining participation later in adolescence if youth are not involved during the early adolescent years.[60]

In her foundational study of religious youth programs in the United States, Kenda Creasy Dean identifies several basic types of programming offered by congregations and other youth religious youth organizations, which are adapted here.

YOUTH GROUPS

Youth groups, Dean writes, are "a club-like gathering of young people who typically meet for socializing, study, community service, and worship experiences together."[61] Not only is this the basic unit in most congregational youth programming among both Christians and Jews, but it is also the format used in most para-congregation organizations and community-based independent Jewish youth organizations such as B'nai B'rith. Youth groups often meet during the week and have special trips and social activities.

FORMAL INSTRUCTION

Congregations almost always adopt a more formal education setting to accomplish more explicitly educational tasks such as the study of scripture (in, for example, Sunday school), music programs (especially choir), preparation for membership (bar/bat mitzvah or confirmation), or learning Hebrew (in Hebrew school).[62]

RECREATION

Though generally connected to religious youth groups, well-developed recreation programs are widespread within some traditions, most notably Southern Baptist. Individual congregations may have youth basketball, softball, and other teams that compete locally, regionally, and even nationally with other religious youth programs.

WORSHIP

Often public worship is the primary context for integrating youth into the intergenerational community of faith. In some congregations, youth have active roles as leaders in these settings. However, Dean found that many religious youth leaders do not consider worship to be part of youth work at all. Jewish leaders place far less emphasis on worship involvement as a structure for youth programming that do those in many Christian traditions.[63]

AFTER-SCHOOL PROGRAMS

A growing number of religious congregations sponsor after-school programs, particularly for fifth- and sixth-grade youth. Some of these programs are developed locally. Others sponsor national programs such as the Logos Program or Pioneer Clubs. In addition, many congregations sponsor Boy Scout, Girl Scout, or Camp Fire groups both for youth in the congregation and the community.

RESIDENTIAL EXPERIENCES

Residential experiences include the camps, conferences (regional and national), retreats, trips, and other "events" that have become the backbone of many youth programs among both Jews and Christians. These are described by Dean as "one of the most powerful community structures in religious youth programs."[64] The strength of relationships that can form in these experiences often mean they reach and include youth who are not already active in the sponsoring congregation.

LEADERSHIP DEVELOPMENT

Some denominations and congregations have programs designed specifically to create a cadre of youth who serve as leaders for youth programming—and as future leaders for the religious community itself. These may include local congregation councils, advisory groups for regional bodies, or elected youth representatives to the national structure. Teenagers involved in these programs often spend more than ten hours a week on religious youth-related activities.

COMMUNITY CENTERS

Uniquely available to Jewish youth, community centers "stand at the center of the Jewish community to bring together Jews, regardless of synagogue-affiliation, for the purpose of promoting Jewish culture and interaction with other Jews."[65] Trained workers develop relationships with Jewish adolescents and maintain important contact with Jewish youth after their bar/bat mitzvahs, when many Jewish youth drop out of synagogue life.

While the Jewish Community Centers are unique in their focus, it is also important to note that many congregations (or groups of congregations) sponsor community youth outreach centers that seek to provide positive recreation for youth and to draw youth into the faith. These are most common in independent evangelical traditions and in urban areas.

PAROCHIAL SCHOOLS

Some religious traditions (most notably Roman Catholic, Seventh-Day Adventist, and Lutheran Church–Missouri Synod) see parochial education as a major outreach to youth. In these schools, they seek to provide a quality education for young people within the context and values of their faith tradition. Religious instruction is at the core of the curriculum, influencing all subject areas.

Because parochial schools face a vast array of unique issues and opportunities, this paper does not seek to address the issues within this school context. However, principles of youth development noted here would also be relevant to the parochial school context.

FIGURE 5.1

YOUTH PROGRAMMING OFFERED IN MAINLINE PROTESTANT CONGREGATIONS

The following chart shows the percentages of mainline Protestant congregations in which the coordinator of religious education says the congregation offers each program or event in the current year.

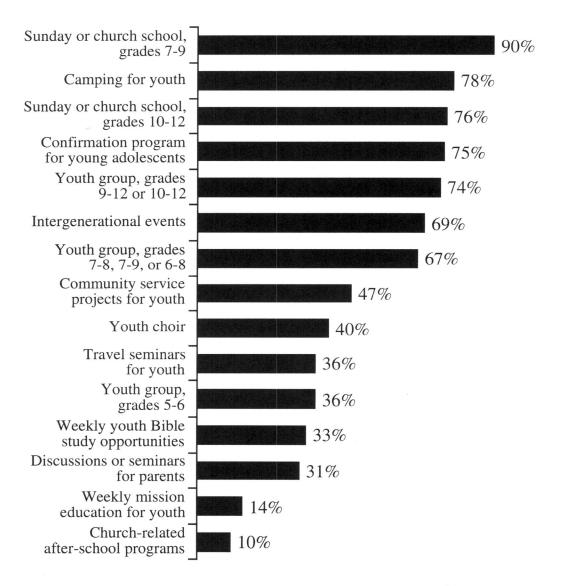

Program	Percentage
Sunday or church school, grades 7-9	90%
Camping for youth	78%
Sunday or church school, grades 10-12	76%
Confirmation program for young adolescents	75%
Youth group, grades 9-12 or 10-12	74%
Intergenerational events	69%
Youth group, grades 7-8, 7-9, or 6-8	67%
Community service projects for youth	47%
Youth choir	40%
Travel seminars for youth	36%
Youth group, grades 5-6	36%
Weekly youth Bible study opportunities	33%
Discussions or seminars for parents	31%
Weekly mission education for youth	14%
Church-related after-school programs	10%

Based on Effective Christian Education: A National Study of Protestant Congregations.[66]

PROGRAM FREQUENCY

Dean's typology usefully captures the range of programs offered by congregations and other religious institutions. Figures 5.1 and 5.2 show percentages of congregations offering various types of programs. Figure 5.1 draws from Search Institute's 1990 study of mainline Protestant congregations.

The 1995 study of youth workers—which includes a broad range of Christian faith traditions and denominations, and a small number of Jewish respondents—also found that formal religious instruction is by far the most common type of program offered (Figure 5.2). Other types of programs occur infrequently, if at all. According to youth workers, the great majority of youth rarely experience in their congregations the following: community service projects, leadership development opportunities, discussions of sexuality, or special programs targeted to the prevention of negative behaviors.

LEADERSHIP IN RELIGIOUS YOUTH PROGRAMS

One could argue that both the strength and weakness of religious youth work is its leadership. On the one hand, religious youth programs involve thousands of concerned and dedicated volunteers who care about young people. Leaders at four levels impact the quality and shape of youth programming: clergy, religious education coordinators, professional youth workers, and volunteer youth workers. The first three groups make up an estimated 20 percent of youth workers, with 80 percent being volunteers.[67] In the 1995 study, volunteers comprise 60 percent of the sample; two-thirds of the youth workers work only part-time. Among paid youth workers, 32 percent work part time; among volunteers, 90 percent work part time.

CLERGY

Whether or not they are directly involved in youth work, pastors and rabbis have an influential role as leaders of their congregations. Furthermore, many youth programs in small congregations rely on clergy to provide their only consistent leadership. Dean concluded that African American clergy exhibit more interest and involvement in youth work than white clergy.[68]

RELIGIOUS EDUCATORS

Youth work is often considered a sub-unit of a larger religious education program. In these cases, a director of religious education may have oversight for youth programming, as well as educational programming for other ages.

FIGURE 5.2 — PERCENT OF CONGREGATIONS THAT REGULARLY OFFER VARIOUS TYPES OF PROGRAMMING

The following chart shows the percentages of religious youth workers who say their congregation offers each program.

	WEEKLY OR MORE	1-2 TIMES PER MONTH	ONCE OR SEVERAL TIMES PER YEAR	NEVER
Formal religious instruction	78%	7%	11%	5%
Youth group	53%	35%	9%	3%
Scripture study group	39%	14%	19%	29%
Youth choir	35%	10%	15%	41%
Recreation	22%	49%	27%	13%
Youth worship services	14%	12%	57%	17%
Leadership development	3%	5%	45%	48%
Mission projects	2%	4%	69%	26%
Community service projects	1%	9%	76%	14%
Prevention programs	1%	1%	40%	58%
Residential experiences (camps, retreats, etc.)	1%	2%	91%	7%
Discussions of sexuality	1%	3%	70%	26%
Regional/national gatherings	<1%	1%	74%	24%
Trips to religious locations	0%	<1%	6%	94%

* Numbers may not add to 100 percent due to rounding.

Based on Search Institute's 1995 study *The Attitudes and Needs of Religious Youth Workers: Perspectives from the Field.*

PROFESSIONAL YOUTH WORKERS

Professional youth workers (who may or may not be ordained) provide the foundation for religious youth work. They may serve full or part time in youth work, and they may also have responsibility for other areas of work (such as family and/or children's education).

Professionals are the primary consumers of the major youth education periodicals and national training by denominations and independent organizations. However, for many, youth work is considered a "stepping stone" to other positions that have more prestige and compensation. As a result, turnover among professional workers tends to be high.

It is impossible to find reliable statistics on youth worker tenure. By some estimates, the average youth worker tenure in Protestant congregations is two and a half years. Among Jewish youth workers, it is thought to be about 18 months.[69] A survey of *Group Magazine* readers (largely evangelical and mainline Christian) found that they have been in their positions an average of two and a half years. The same survey found that the average youth worker has been involved in youth work for nine years.[70]

In our 1995 study, half the sample of both paid youth workers and volunteers have worked with their current congregation for three or fewer years. More than one-third of that sample have spent 11 years or more in religious youth work, but nearly one-quarter have spent three or fewer years doing youth work in a congregation.

VOLUNTEER YOUTH WORKERS

Volunteers are the life blood of religious youth programs. In some cases (small congregations and most non-white congregations), a volunteer carries full responsibility for developing and managing the youth program. In our 1995 survey, 42 percent of volunteer youth workers said they are responsible for running their youth program. In addition, volunteers carry out most of the programming, even in programs with professional leadership.

TRAINING

In general, anyone can serve as a youth worker; rarely are any qualifications or training required, though individual congregations may have strong volunteer training programs and opportunities. Among the volunteer youth workers surveyed in 1995, 51 percent said they have received no training for their responsibilities in the past year, compared to 46 percent of paid staff. As Figure 5.3 shows, other training differences between paid and volunteer youth workers include:

- Paid staff are more likely to have received college-, seminary- or graduate-level training for youth work. They are also more likely to have been part of a youth work internship.

- Volunteers are more likely to receive their training within their congregation.

FIGURE 5.3   **TRAINING EXPERIENCES OF PROFESSIONAL AND VOLUNTEER YOUTH WORKERS**

(Percent of religious youth workers reporting each type of training specifically for youth work.)

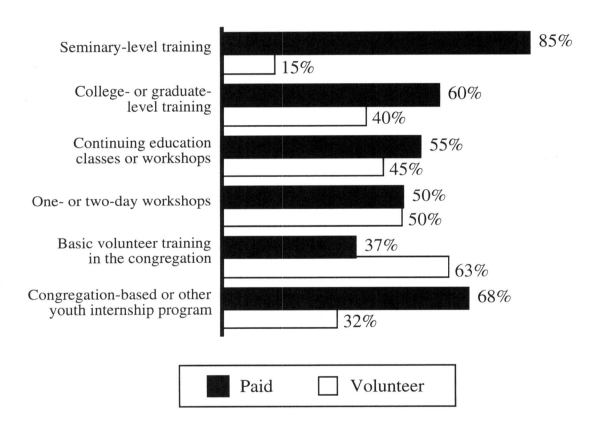

Based on Search Institute's 1995 study *The Attitudes and Needs of Religious Youth Workers: Perspectives from the Field.*

It is difficult to know exactly how many youth are involved in religious youth programs. Surveys tend to report that about half of all youth are connected to a church or synagogue. However, this measure includes those who attend worship services only.[71] A variety of studies suggest that about one-third of youth are connected to congregations outside of weekly services:

- The National Education Longitudinal Study of 1988 found that 34 percent of adolescents are part of religious youth groups.[72]

- Similarly, a 1991 Gallup Youth Survey found that 41 percent of American youth go to Sunday school and 36 percent belong to a congregational youth group.[73]

THE DROPOUT FACTOR

However, averages for all teenagers hide the higher levels of involvement of young adolescents. For example, Search Institute research has found that 52 percent of seventh- to ninth-grade youth connected to mainline Protestant congregations are involved in religious education, compared to 35 percent of 10th- to 12th-grade youth.[74] Percentages from various parallel studies in different denominations are cited in Figure 5.4.

In the 1995 survey, only 7 percent of religious youth workers said they have "a lot" of trouble keeping fifth and sixth graders involved, 12 percent do with seventh to ninth graders. But 55 percent have a lot of trouble keeping 10th to 12th graders involved.

Religious leaders see a shift to higher proportions of involvement of younger rather than older adolescents, estimating that between 50 and 75 percent of youth in denominational youth programs are under age 15.[75] Furthermore, this trend also reflects the problem of young people who drop out of the youth program after completing membership classes.

Current involvement trends suggest, in Dean's words, that "religious youth work is at a crossroads in American Protestant, Catholic, and Jewish communities. On the one hand, these communities are serving adolescents in more ways than ever before; on the other hand, fewer adolescents are actively involved in the corporate life of the religious community than a generation ago."[76] Patterns are slightly different in each major tradition:[77]

- Mainline Protestants have seen a steady decline in youth work (and in overall influence nationally) since the 1950s.

FIGURE 5.4   YOUTH INVOLVEMENT IN CONGREGATIONS IN SEVERAL CHRISTIAN DENOMINATIONS

GRADE (AGE)	MAINLINE PROTESTANT*[78]			SEVENTH-DAY ADVENTIST[79]			LUTHERAN CHURCH-MISSOURI SYNOD[80]		
	7th	9th	12th	7th	9th	12th	Age 13	Age 15	Age 17
Attend religious services at least weekly	68%	65%	59%	73%	78%	77%	84%	75%	72%
Attend programs or events other than worship*	64%	62%	50%	54%	54%	48%	58%	51%	46%
Volunteer to lead, teach, or serve in the congregation*	21%	32%	33%	25%	21%	22%	30%	34%	35%
Participate in religious program outside congregation*	28%	32%	24%	n/a	n/a	n/a	34%	28%	34%

*Three or more hours in the past month.

- Conservative evangelical congregations have seen modest growth that now appears to be stabilizing.

- Catholics made a major commitment to youth ministry in the 1980s, but have more recently experienced major financial cutbacks.

- Jewish youth programs (including educational programs such as supplementary schools and day schools) has remained relatively stable. Participation in synagogue-based programs appears to have declined in the past decade.[81]

- Evangelical parachurch organizations saw steady increases through the 1980s, but more recently have faced financial cutbacks. Several national parachurch groups have been on the verge of bankruptcy and are undergoing major change.[82]

THE IMPACT OF RELIGIOUS YOUTH PROGRAMS

While the exact nature of adolescents' involvement is unclear across the spectrum of faith traditions, there is solid evidence that something positive happens to young people that is connected to their religious involvement.

RISKY BEHAVIORS

An analysis of data from *The Troubled Journey* found that youth involved in religious settings are half as likely as uninvolved youth to display many "at-risk" behaviors. For example, here are percentages of sixth- to 12th-grade public school students who are at risk in various areas, depending on whether they are involved in religious activities[83].

Percent at risk in . . .[84]	High Involvement in Religious Activities	Low Involvement in Religious Activities
Binge drinking	7%	15%
Problem drug use	5%	14%
Sexual intercourse	22%	42%
Attempted suicide	10%	17%[85]

It should be noted, however, that religious involvement does not inoculate youth against these behaviors. For example, Search Institute's study of mainline Protestant youth found that 74 percent are involved in at least one at-risk behavior out of a set of ten. (One-third are involved in three or more.) Even among youth who are highly active in their faith communities, 71 percent are engaged in at least one of these behaviors.[86]

A study of Seventh-Day Adventist youth using the same scale found that 60 percent of sixth-grade youth and 73 percent of 12th-grade youth (in a tradition with strict moral and health codes) are involved in at least one of the at-risk behaviors.[87]

The Seventh-Day Adventist data give clues to congregational characteristics that may be influencing these behaviors. Multiple regression analysis found that the following two congregational variables were most associated with lower levels of at-risk involvement among youth in grades six to eight:

- Perceptions that the teachers and leaders in the church are warm and accepting; and

- Frequency of church attendance.

When combined with other variables (including the influences of family and school), perceptions of teachers remain the second-most powerful variable, exceeded only by "the quality of family worship."[88] Further research is needed to know whether these same or similar correlations hold true in other faith traditions.

PROSOCIAL BEHAVIOR   The research is even less clear in connecting religious involvement and prosocial behaviors. However, there is some empirical evidence that religious involvement and commitment do lead young people to develop prosocial attitudes and behaviors. For example, analysis of data from *The Troubled Journey* reveals meaningful connections between religious activity and caring attitudes and behaviors. Interestingly, this analysis found that the importance a young person places on religion is a better predictor of caring than is religious involvement, as shown in Figure 5.5.

While 55 percent of youth who say religion is not important have caring attitudes, 86 percent of those who say religion is "very important" express a caring attitude. An even greater difference is seen in the area of caring activity, jumping from 29 percent of youth who say religion is not important to 60 percent of those who say it is very important.

Other studies of religious adolescents also find that they place a priority on caring for others. A study of Jewish youth in Tucson, for example, found that such interests rank in their top ten.[89] Dean concludes: "These patterns of altruism, if not caused by religious communities, are at least consistent with their teachings."[90]

FIGURE 5.5 — THE RELATIONSHIP BETWEEN RELIGION AND CARING AMONG SIXTH- TO EIGHTH-GRADE PUBLIC SCHOOL STUDENTS[91]

	PERCENT OF TOTAL	CARING ATTITUDE*	SERVICE INVOLVEMENT**
CHURCH/SYNAGOGUE ATTENDANCE			
Never	18%	62%	32%
Rarely	24%	70%	41%
Once or twice a month	14%	72%	48%
About once a week or more	44%	75%	55%
IMPORTANCE OF RELIGION			
Not important	2%	55%	29%
Somewhat important	27%	66%	42%
Important	45%	75%	51%
Very important	26%	86%	60%

* Percent who place importance on "helping other people."

** Percent who report that they have "helped people who are poor, hungry, sick, or unable to care for themselves," once or more in the past 12 months.

Based on a sample of 47,000 sixth- to 12th-grade students in public schools

To say that religious youth programs have "potential" for youth development fails to give them adequate credit for the instrumental role the religious community has played in the formation of youth work in this country. In her summary of the history of youth work in the United States, Judith Erickson notes that many of the major national youth development efforts have religious roots (for example, YMCA and YWCA). Indeed, in 1831, a church spawned the first national activities intentionally designed to involve youth when the First Reformed Presbyterian Church of Philadelphia organized the Juvenile Mission Society.[92]

Furthermore, religious youth programs remain a formidable force on the national scene. In Erickson's *Directory of American Youth Organizations,* one out of three organizations is a religious organization—and the listing doesn't include major denominations or the thousands of congregational and independent programs across the country.[93]

Yet these historical notes and statistics are sometimes forgotten, both in the religious community and in the larger field of youth work. Thus it is useful to gather together the multitude of factors that underscore the strength that religious organizations can bring to a positive youth development approach.

COMPATIBLE MISSION   Across the theological spectrum, religious youth programs seem surprisingly united in their commitment to the healthy development of young people. Dean writes:

> *Despite the diversity of theologies, polities, histories, and programs which inform religious youth work in the 1990s, religious youth programs share remarkably similar goals and assumptions, which, while often unspoken, direct their work with adolescents. . . . [T]hese programs assume the need to envelop young people, usually their own, in a caring community that will facilitate adolescent development and see them safely into adulthood as mature, productive members of society.[94]*

To illustrate, a six-denomination study by Dean Hoge and his colleagues found that two of the four goals most frequently endorsed by parents and religious educators for religious education and youth programming are developmental objectives: "Has a healthy self-concept about his or her value and worthiness as a person" and "Takes a responsible view toward moral questions such as drug use and sex behavior."[95]

On a programmatic level, religious education coordinators in mainline Protestant congregations were asked to identify their congregations' priorities for work with youth. Four of the five highest emphases can all be seen to have an explicit positive youth development component:

- Providing fellowship or social interaction (70 percent)

- Learning how to apply faith to life (66 percent)

- Teaching moral values (60 percent)

- Teaching moral decision-making (60 percent)

- Developing Bible knowledge (50 percent)[96]

Similarly, in Search Institute's 1995 study, most of the most important goals for religious youth programs involved positive youth development and are goals shared by many secular youth-serving organizations. (See Figure 5.6.)

Dean suggests that several assumptions underlie religious organizations' commitment to the healthy development of youth:

- Religious youth programs recognize that faith is not a shield against hardship, but it does have a protective influence against at-risk behaviors.

- Religious youth workers believe that religious experience is, itself, a fundamental developmental need.

- Finally, religious youth workers believe that the support of a caring community is essential to positive development, and the faith community is in a position to provide that support. As Dean writes: "The experience of 'connectedness' is not merely a spiritual phenomenon; it translates into caring for the entire community with which one is connected."[97]

Thus—unlike in schools where shifts in thinking are necessary for educators to begin accepting their role in youth development—the majority of the religious community appears to be already committed to such a goal. Excerpts from mission statements and other documents from national religious denominations illustrate these groups' commitment to youth development as a goal of religious youth work.

FIGURE 5.6

YOUTH WORKERS' PERCEPTIONS OF THE MOST IMPORTANT GOALS FOR THEIR PROGRAMS

The following chart shows the percentages of religious youth workers who consider each goal to be "very important" for their congregational youth program.

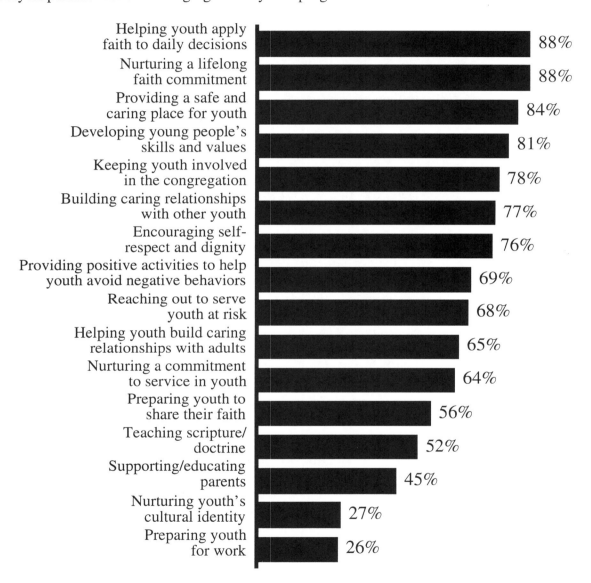

Helping youth apply faith to daily decisions	88%
Nurturing a lifelong faith commitment	88%
Providing a safe and caring place for youth	84%
Developing young people's skills and values	81%
Keeping youth involved in the congregation	78%
Building caring relationships with other youth	77%
Encouraging self-respect and dignity	76%
Providing positive activities to help youth avoid negative behaviors	69%
Reaching out to serve youth at risk	68%
Helping youth build caring relationships with adults	65%
Nurturing a commitment to service in youth	64%
Preparing youth to share their faith	56%
Teaching scripture/ doctrine	52%
Supporting/educating parents	45%
Nurturing youth's cultural identity	27%
Preparing youth for work	26%

Based on Search Institute's 1995 study *The Attitudes and Needs of Religious Youth Workers: Perspectives from the Field.*

Orthodox—"The primary responsibility for the upbringing of young people rests with their parents. But the Church, too, has always had an important helping role in the spiritual, personal, and social growth of youth. This role is all the more urgent, albeit all the more difficult, in our own age because of the nature of secular and pluralistic society.[98]

Roman Catholic—"Youth ministry is a multidimensional reality, but all of its varied facets are brought into focus by a common dedication to the following goals. 1. Youth ministry works to foster the total personal and spiritual growth of each young person. 2. Youth ministry seeks to draw young people to responsible participation in the life, mission and work of the faith community."[99]

Southern Baptist—A series of 16 "Youth Ministry Objectives" were developed by youth-related personnel in the agencies and institutions of the Southern Baptist Convention "to guide professional and volunteer youth workers." These objectives include: "To help youth grow in understanding and acceptance of self. . . . To guide youth to explore their abilities and talents and develop a Christian perspective on choosing a vocation. . . . To guide youth to develop good habits in the constructive use of their leisure time. . . . To offer youth opportunities for Christian fellowship and the development of social skills."[100]

At the same time, it is important to note that this commitment is not always explicit or clearly articulated. Several mission statements received from national offices include no clear commitment to youth development, though examinations of the specific programs shows that programs do include youth development components.[101]

ACCESS TO FAMILIES

Congregations have a great opportunity to influence young people by influencing their families. Seventy percent of American adults claim to be affiliated with a religious congregation, according to Gallup Surveys.[102] And though only about 40 percent of adults attend services weekly, 58 percent of all adults (and 54 percent of adults ages 30-49) claim to attend church or synagogue at least monthly.[103] Thus, a large percentage of youth have parents who are connected to religious congregations.

Furthermore, one of the common reasons young adults return to religious involvement after dropping out is for the sake of their children. Another Gallup survey asked adults who had become more active in religious activities to state the reasons for their increased involvement. Out of 34 possible responses, "for our children" and "now have a stronger faith and beliefs" were the two most commonly cited reasons.[104] And, finally, a

Gallup report titled *The Unchurched American: Ten Years Later* found that 73 percent of adults who are not connected to congregations still want their children to receive religious instruction.[105]

This increased interest in religious activities among parents presents an important opportunity for religious organizations to reach families. Through relevant parent education and support programs, religious organizations can enhance parents' abilities to be responsible sources of support, control, and values for youth.

CARING LEADERS

Since caring relationships with adults are at the heart of positive youth development, religious organizations have particular strength in the care and commitment of their professional and volunteer leaders. In mainline Protestant denominations, 79 percent of youth say leaders care about them.[106]

INTERGENERATIONAL COMMUNITY

In an age-segmented society, congregations remain one of the few settings in which many youth could have regular opportunities for formal and informal contact with principled, caring adults of all ages. About 83 percent of 7th and 8th grade Protestant youth say four or more adults in the congregation know them well. In addition, 85 percent indicate that there is at least one adult in their congregation who they would feel comfortable going to for help if they had an important question about their life.[107] Youth workers in such settings have the opportunity to employ such contacts for the transmission of important life values.

SERVICE EMPHASIS

All major faith traditions include an emphasis on service as a part of the faith, and many congregations make service an integral part of their youth program. According to an Independent Sector survey, youth are about twice as likely to learn about possible volunteer activities through their religious congregations (62 percent) than any other organization, including schools (34 percent).[108]

VALUES BASE

Schools and non-sectarian organizations increasingly are confronting values head-on, but most still shy from explicit discussions of values. In contrast, shaping values is at the core of the congregation's mission. By nurturing positive values, congregations help to shape the life choices of the young people they touch. These values can become a foundation for discussions of the life choices young people face regarding sexuality, and alcohol and other drugs, and other current issues and concerns.

COMPETENCIES

By giving young people leadership and responsibility—in youth programs, congregations, and denominational structures—religious organizations cultivate important social competencies. This growth occurs as youth do things such as plan their own programs, lead in the congregation, become peer ministers, take responsibility for caring for younger children, and help to shape the direction and future of their denomination.

COMMUNITY LEADERSHIP

Though it is often ignored as a partner in national efforts on behalf of youth, the religious community provides critical leadership to communities—particularly in the African American community. "Americans are more likely to belong to a congregation than any other voluntary organization," says Nancy Ammerman. "In many communities, congregations are among the most significant players in community affairs."[109] Using this position of leadership in the community can make congregations the guiding force behind community-wide efforts to shape programs and services from a youth development perspective.

CHALLENGES TO ADDRESS IN BUILDING ASSETS THROUGH CONGREGATIONS

While it is clear that most congregations are committed to the healthy development of young people and have tremendous potential in this area, the reality does not always match the mission. Too often, congregations reflect the negative perspective on youth that permeates society at large. Furthermore, too many congregations simply neglect the real issues young people face. Children's Defense Fund Founder Marian Wright Edelman articulates the problem starkly:

> *Churches [and synagogues] ought to be the moral locomotives speaking out about [youth issues], and they are the caboose. . . . In many ways, we're scared of our kids. We hear many of our ministers talk about adolescents as is they are the enemy or the other. It's tragic. We have abandoned our children in fundamental ways.*[110]

In addition to the gaps in addressing larger youth issues, there is evidence that congregations do not always meet the needs of the young people they directly involve. Figure 5.7 shows the percentages of seventh- to 12th-grade youth who say their congregation does a good or excellent job in a variety of areas related to positive development, according to Search Institute's study of mainline Protestant congregations. The study found:

- Only 43 percent of church youth say they receive care and support from adults in church (six or more times in the past year).

FIGURE 5.7

ADOLESCENTS' RATINGS OF THEIR CONGREGATIONS' EFFECTIVENESS IN ADDRESSING YOUTH DEVELOPMENT ISSUES

This chart shows the percentage of mainline Protestant youth who say their congregation does a good or excellent job in each area.[111]

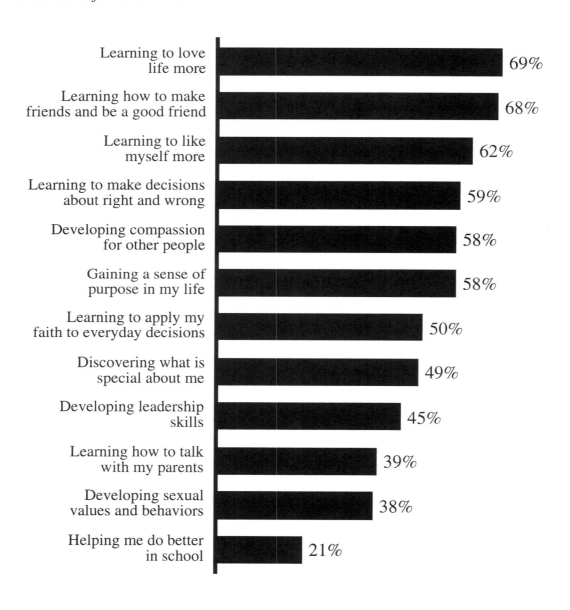

Learning to love life more	69%
Learning how to make friends and be a good friend	68%
Learning to like myself more	62%
Learning to make decisions about right and wrong	59%
Developing compassion for other people	58%
Gaining a sense of purpose in my life	58%
Learning to apply my faith to everyday decisions	50%
Discovering what is special about me	49%
Developing leadership skills	45%
Learning how to talk with my parents	39%
Developing sexual values and behaviors	38%
Helping me do better in school	21%

- Just 40 percent say their congregation does a good or excellent job of getting them involved in helping other people.

- Only 49 percent say they learn a lot at church.

- About 46 percent wish their congregation offered more for people their age.[112]

In Search Institute's 1995 study, there were large gaps between the proportion of youth workers who believe various goals are very important for youth programs and the proportion who think they are achieving them well, as Figure 5.8 displays.

As we would expect, several faith-specific goals are top priorities and, even with these priorities gaps are large. In addition, however, several youth development goals are also rated "very important" by most youth workers, and the gaps between importance and achievement is substantial.

A gap between mission and practice in working with young adolescents is not unique to religious organizations. Though tremendous energy and resources have been put into middle school restructuring and reform, studies generally find that most changes that occur are superficial and that most schools are still not responsive to young people's needs.[113]

Several programmatic challenges, attitudes, and societal issues limit religious organizations' effectiveness in youth development.

LIMITED TRAINING

One challenge lies in the fact that religious youth workers—an estimated 60 to 80 percent of whom are volunteers—rarely receive any training. "The vast majority of youth workers' training," writes Dean, "is a talk with their predecessor and a few weeks on-the-job." [114] In her research, Dean found that, while some training is available for youth workers, it is often inaccessible to volunteers—and there is not enough of it. There is a particularly severe shortage of training for religious youth workers in high-risk or ethnically diverse environments.[115]

In our 1995 study, less than one-third of religious youth workers had been trained to work with youth in seminary or college-level courses. Most relied on one or two-day workshops, but half of the sample had received no training in the previous year. (Also see Figure 5.3.)

What training is available tends to focus more heavily on doctrinal and faith issues. Youth workers, particularly volunteers, are much less likely to be trained in the broader context of young people's lives and development

FIGURE 5.8

YOUTH PROGRAM GOALS: GAP BETWEEN IMPORTANCE AND ACHIEVEMENT

The following table shows the gap between how important youth workers say each goal is and how well they achieve it (ranked from largest to smallest gap).

GOAL	IMPORTANCE (Percent who say goal is "very important")	ACHIEVEMENT (Percent who say program does "very well")	GAP BETWEEN IMPORTANCE AND ACHIEVEMENT
Nurturing a life-long faith commitment	88%	22%	66%
Helping youth apply faith to daily decisions	88%	25%	63%
Reaching out to serve at-risk youth	68%	9%	59%
Developing youth skills and values	81%	24%	57%
Keeping youth involved in the congregation	78%	21%	57%
Building caring relationships with other youth	77%	30%	47%
Preparing youth to share their faith	56%	12%	44%
Nurturing a commitment to service	64%	22%	42%
Encouraging self-respect and dignity	76%	35%	41%
Building caring relationships with adults	65%	25%	40%
Supporting and educating parents	45%	6%	38%
Teaching scripture and doctrine	52%	22%	30%
Providing positive activities to help youth avoid negative behaviors	69%	43%	26%
Preparing youth for work	26%	4%	22%
Providing a safe and caring place for youth	84%	64%	20%
Nurturing young people's cultural identity	27%	10%	17%

Based on Search Institute's 1995 study *The Attitudes and Needs of Religious Youth Workers: Perspectives from the Field.*

and in the methods and structures that enhance that healthy development. In her research, Dean identified only two training programs designed to train religious youth workers in young adolescent development, both of which are strong, but require intensive commitments.[116]

Search Institute's 1995 analysis of the training and resources in youth development offered by 34 national religious and secular organizations found that while some elements of positive youth development programming are addressed, there are almost no resources or trainings that use a comprehensive framework (such as asset building) as a unifying model. Moreover, some of the key areas that youth workers identify as very important program goals—such as decision making and development of youth leadership—are not well-represented in available trainings and resources.

Youth workers seem well aware of this situation. Our training and resource review found youth decision making to be one of the least well-covered areas. At the same time, the number one topic in which youth workers are very interested in more training and resources for helping youth make positive life choices. Given our overall findings, it is promising that about half or more of religious youth workers in our survey are very interested in training and materials in key youth development areas, as shown in Figure 5.9.

LOW PRIORITY ON YOUTH WORK

Youth work is rarely a major congregational priority, particularly among mainline Protestant denominations. To illustrate, Dean cites a Lilly Endowment study from the 1970s that found that 95 percent of theological seminaries call youth work a critical problem of the church, but just 5 percent of these same institutions are addressing the need.[117] The only denomination Dean identified that makes youth work a national priority is the Church of Jesus Christ of the Latter-Day Saints.[118]

In the Search Institute survey of religious youth workers, half of the youth workers say congregational support for youth is just fair or even poor, as reflected in budgets, providing volunteer or paid staff for youth programs, and the overall priority of youth programs. Perhaps most telling: Just 43 percent say they have a clear mission statement for their youth program.

LIMITED RESOURCES

Because youth work is rarely a high priority in denominations, resources such as time, finances, and personnel are all in short supply. "Except in conservative evangelical Christian traditions, where support for youth work is high, religious communities are more apt to pay lip service than

FIGURE 5.9

RELIGIOUS YOUTH WORKERS' INTERESTS IN YOUTH DEVELOPMENT TRAINING AND MATERIALS

This chart shows the percentage of religious youth workers surveyed who are "very interested" in training and resources in each topic area.

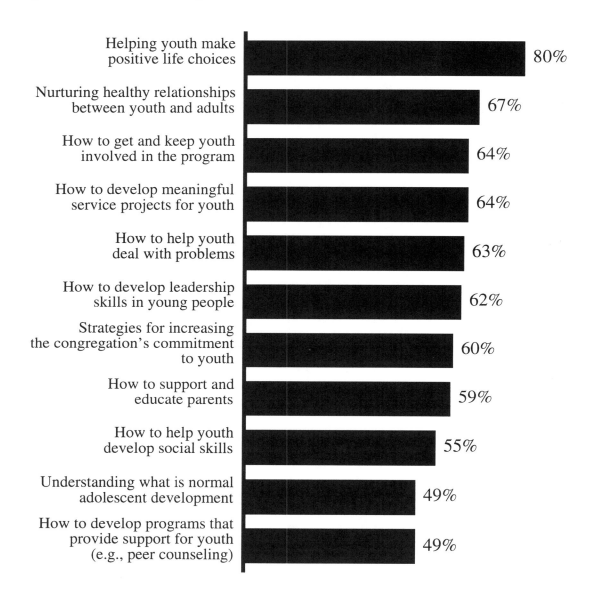

Helping youth make positive life choices — 80%

Nurturing healthy relationships between youth and adults — 67%

How to get and keep youth involved in the program — 64%

How to develop meaningful service projects for youth — 64%

How to help youth deal with problems — 63%

How to develop leadership skills in young people — 62%

Strategies for increasing the congregation's commitment to youth — 60%

How to support and educate parents — 59%

How to help youth develop social skills — 55%

Understanding what is normal adolescent development — 49%

How to develop programs that provide support for youth (e.g., peer counseling) — 49%

Based on Search Institute's 1995 study *The Attitudes and Needs of Religious Youth Workers: Perspectives from the Field.*

bills for those who work with adolescents," Dean concludes.[119] A report on Jewish education illustrates the problem:

> *Were cost not a factor, Jewish communities might provide a profusion of Jewish educational experiences for the broadest possible spectrum of American Jews. However, the costs of Jewish education are substantial. . . . Jewish institutions, agencies, synagogues, and communities make hard choices about what types of education— supplementary schools, one-day-a-week schools, day schools, Jewish camps, Israel trips, etc.—should be offered , to whom, and at what price.[120]*

Operating with limited resources affects religious youth work at all levels. Salaries for professional youth workers are low—one factor that reduces the number of religious professionals who choose long-term careers in youth work. Local youth programs often cannot afford to offer adequate training and resources for volunteers. Finally, most denominational support structures for youth work have also experienced multiple cutbacks, limiting the assistance and training these organizations provide.

INADEQUATE MATERIALS While materials specifically for religious education are plentiful (particularly from a conservative evangelical perspective), support materials around issues of youth development (except, perhaps, for community service projects) are almost non-existent. With the exception of the largest denominations, most do not have large enough constituencies to allow them to develop their own extensive youth work publications and training programs (programs for which denominational subsidies have dried up).

This gap is less problematic for evangelical and mainline Christian groups who easily borrow and adapt from each other. Those from less dominant faith traditions have a more difficult problem. David Frank, Director of the North American Federation of Temple Youth, puts it this way:

> *We have to produce all program resources through our denominational offices. . . . Resources are gobbled up faster than we can produce them. We have no publication house; there are not enough of us to make such publications possible. We adapt what we have to.[121]*

DIFFERENT GOALS All major religious traditions in the United States recognize and affirm the importance of the healthy development of young people. As we noted earlier, most see this as an important aspect of youth work. Less clear, however, is the relationship between faith/cultural nurture (learning the doctrine and traditions of the faith) and positive youth development. Figure 5.10 suggests different ways the two goals can be related:

1. **Faith/cultural identity is a subset of youth development**—This perspective would hold that the primary goal is the healthy overall development of youth. Faith/cultural identity is secondary in importance. This model would probably be the dominant image among social scientists and more liberal religious traditions.

2. **Youth development is a subset of faith/cultural identity**—For the majority of religious youth workers, faith/cultural identity is the focal point of youth work; everything else can be subsumed into this central goal. As Dean writes:

   Whereas developmental psychology suggests that major arenas of identity formation include selecting and preparing for a future career, working out a political ideology, adopting a set of social roles, and reevaluating religious and moral beliefs, Jewish and Christian theology suggest that this last arena is preeminent. The religious community sees more at stake in religious experience than merely helping the adolescent claim part of her identity; religious experience, says the religious youth worker, is the crucial piece of an adolescent's identity.[122]

3. **Overlapping goals**—Some youth workers believe youth development and faith/cultural identity are overlapping goals, but that some components of youth development are unrelated to faith/cultural identity and vice versa.

4. **Unrelated goals**—For some, faith or cultural identity is distinct from—and even antagonistic toward—adolescent development from a social science perspective. This view might also argue that, in this secular, pluralistic society, the religious community must dedicate all its energy to nurturing faith/cultural identity, since no one else can or will play this role. Individuals with this perspective are potentially the most difficult to involve in efforts to enhance the youth development capacity of religious organizations.

There is strong evidence that faith nurture and youth development are complementary, often employing the same methods in reaching their distinct goals. In its Effective Christian Education study, Search Institute identified characteristics of religious education programs that are most associated with growth in faith among youth. Of the 15 factors identified as important, 12 are directly or indirectly related to positive youth development (see Figure 5.11). The problem is that many of these characteristics are not in place in most congregations.

FIGURE 5.10

IMAGES OF THE RELATIONSHIP BETWEEN YOUTH DEVELOPMENT AND RELIGIOUS/FAITH IDENTITY

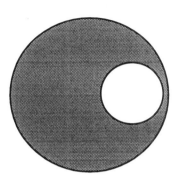

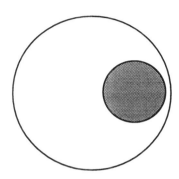

1. Faith/cultural identity is a subset of positive youth development

2. Youth development is a subset of faith/cultural identity

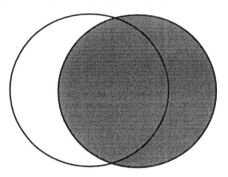

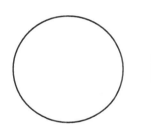

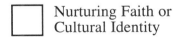
3. Overlapping goals

4. Unrelated goals

☐ Nurturing Faith or Cultural Identity

▓ Positive Youth Development

Similarly, as we have seen, positive youth development goals dominated the list of goals religious youth workers in the 1995 study feel are important, but few goals are considered well-achieved.

THEOLOGICAL CONFLICTS   While there may be wide agreement that healthy development is an important element of religious youth work, some religious traditions (particularly those that are theologically conservative or fundamentalist) attack some components or emphases of positive youth development as being "secular humanist," "unscriptural," or "unchristian."

Some groups are particularly disturbed by an emphasis on self-development, self-esteem, critical thinking, and other elements that are thought to be human efforts to replace God's power—particularly when these elements are not embedded in religious language or principles.[123]

However, across the theological spectrum, people seem to share a concern about young people and their healthy development. Most seem willing to set aside some differences (if only temporarily) to focus on more effectively caring for youth—particularly when efforts are made to honor their perspective and to use language with which they are comfortable.

Theological differences do play a role in the reluctance of a sizable minority to work with other faiths on behalf of their community's youth. In our 1995 study, we found that about 30 percent are unwilling to collaborate with any other faith tradition but their own on youth issues, and that 22 percent say theological differences are very much a barrier to interfaith collaboration.[124] However, lack of time and scheduling conflicts are considered major barriers by an even number of religious youth workers.

PROBLEM FOCUS   When religious youth programs get involved in youth development issues, they, like others in society, have typically focused attention on the problems. In evangelical Christian programs, the emphasis has generally been on saying no to sex and drugs. African American congregations have been community leaders in efforts against violence, gangs, and drugs.

Limited efforts are directed at preventing specific at-risk behaviors such as suicide, alcohol use, and premature sexual activity (though these topics are rarely addressed directly in most congregations[125]). These issues are most likely to be addressed in a counseling setting.[126] Much less attention has been explicitly focused on enhancing the positive developmental infrastructure for young people.[127]

FIGURE 5.11

FIGURE 5.11 EFFECTIVENESS FACTORS IN YOUTH RELIGIOUS EDUCATION

The following factors have been identified as key factors in religious education programs that effectively nurture faith in seventh- to 12th-grade youth. Percentages represent the mainline Protestant congregations in the United States with each characteristic demonstrated.[128]

FACTORS WITH A HEAVY YOUTH DEVELOPMENT EMPHASIS

Helps develop concern for others	66%
Teaches good friendship skills	65%
Encourages independent thinking and questioning	62%
Creates a sense of community in which people help one another	31%
Emphasizes responsibility for reducing poverty and hunger	30%
Involves youth in service projects	29%
Emphasizes education about human sexuality	27%
Emphasizes education about drugs and alcohol	20%
Emphasizes intergenerational contact	20%

FACTORS THAT BALANCE YOUTH DEVELOPMENT AND A RELIGIOUS FOCUS

Emphasis on moral values and moral decision-making	60%
Helps youth apply faith to daily decisions	49%
Emphasizes life experience as occasion for spiritual insight	36%
Emphasizes the unique unfolding of each person's faith journey	25%

FACTORS WITH AN EXCLUSIVE RELIGIOUS FOCUS

Teaches core theological concepts	74%
Teaches the Bible	66%

LIMITED UNDERSTANDING OF THE SPECIAL NEEDS OF YOUNG ADOLESCENTS

Some evidence suggests that religious programs for young adolescents have increased substantially in the past 15 years. Several major denominations have specific emphases on early adolescent programming, and parachurch organizations (such as Youth for Christ) have developed programs geared for this age group.

However, the quality of these programs and resources remains largely inadequate. In addition, many congregations resist the idea of introducing a youth group model as early as fifth or sixth grade. A survey of readers of *Jr. High Ministry Magazine* found that only 32 percent of the middle-grade programs include sixth graders, and only 4 percent have fifth graders.[129]

Furthermore, while a great deal of attention may be paid to this age group, it is often primarily around religious education and rites of passage such as confirmation and bar/bat mitzvah. And while some of these programs are being reshaped, most do not consciously address young adolescents' developmental needs or learning styles.

YOUTH PROGRAM ISOLATION

While congregations have tremendous potential for surrounding young people with caring relationships with adults of all ages, youth programs tend to be isolated from other areas of congregational life. In many cases, they operate independently from other congregational programs, and the overall programming for young people may be totally separate—including separate worship services. While these approaches may allow for focusing on young people's specific tastes and needs, they also limit the potential of congregations to enhance and encourage intergenerational relationships and to build a sense of youth as valued contributors.

The result is that congregations have difficulty capitalizing on their potential for youth development because they have created an isolated program and youth subculture. Furthermore, congregations are unlikely to make youth work a priority if it is not a visible part of congregational life.

LACK OF FAMILY SUPPORT

We noted earlier that one of the strengths of congregations is their ongoing contact with families. And because of their central role in youth development, this contact should open significant opportunities for congregations to support parents in raising healthy youth.

Despite the potential, however, there is evidence that many congregations have not found effective ways to support and educate parents—or to engage them significantly in the congregation's youth program. In Search Institute's 1990 study, *Effective Christian Education,* only 8 percent of religious education coordinators in mainline Protestant congregations say their congregation emphasizes "providing classes for parents on effective parenting or communication."[130] More recently, a study in The Lutheran Church–Missouri Synod found that only 20 percent of parents say their congregation effectively helps them nurture faith in their children.[131] One can only suspect that even fewer congregations effectively support and educate parents in issues of youth development.

LACK OF ACCESS TO HIGH-RISK YOUTH

Leaders in religious youth work recognize that they typically do not reach young people who are at high risk. "Religious communities tend to perceive at-risk youth to be outside their membership," Dean writes, "and while they recognize the enormous need for services for at-risk adolescents, they are sincerely frustrated at their lack of access, or perceived lack of access, to these teenagers."[132] As we have noted, the Search Institute survey of religious youth workers found that serving at-risk youth is considered a very important goal, but has the largest gap between importance and achievement of any of the goals identified.

Ironically, Figure 5.12 shows that the youth workers in our 1995 survey believe certain non-sectarian activities would be more effective in reaching vulnerable youth, but, as we have noted, their congregations rarely provide these activities.

Virtually all successful religious efforts to reach youth in high-risk communities are local initiatives (with the exception of some successful efforts by the Congress of National Black Churches[133] and national parachurch groups such as Youth for Christ[134]). And while many of these efforts are innovative and effective, they are not widely known, recognized, or supported. The youth workers rarely network together, so they each feel isolated in their work.[135] In addition, resources for these youth workers are virtually non-existent. As an urban youth worker in Chicago complained: "I pick up any magazine, any youth resource, and it's all—100 percent—geared to white kids. . . . Many of the things that are out in youth ministry aren't applicable to the city."[136]

Inadequate attention to young people's cultural backgrounds produces many problems. At the most obvious level, as the youth worker in Chicago notes, the visual presentation of many resources may leave out significant and rapidly growing segments of the youth population, such as Latinos/ Latinas, African Americans, Asians, or Native Americans. In so doing, programs lose the opportunity to draw on cultural strengths such as family and peer support for religious involvement in Latino/Latina and Native American cultures, or the sense of community responsibility for child-

FIGURE 5.12   EFFECTIVE PROGRAMS FOR INVOLVING HARD-TO-REACH YOUTH

The following chart shows the percentages of religious youth workers who believe each type of program would be effective in reaching hard-to-reach youth.

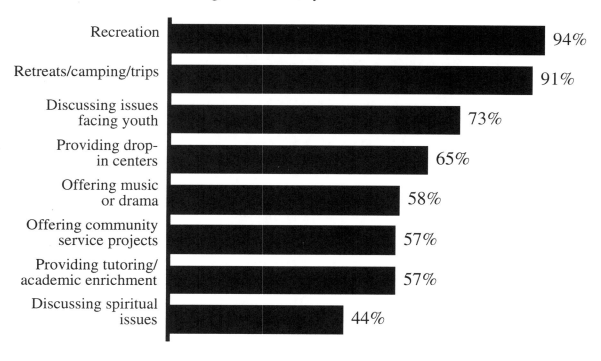

Based on Search Institute's 1995 study *The Attitudes and Needs of Religious Youth Workers: Perspectives from the Field.*

rearing historically common among African American and Native American cultures.

In addition, developing a cultural identity is a critical part of overall identity development, particularly for adolescents of color. Programs which fail to help young people place themselves in a cultural context are therefore less effective. They also miss the opportunity to broaden white youths' understanding of others, and their appreciation of the great variety of heritages represented among white youth.

Unfortunately, our 1995 survey showed that only 27 percent of religious youth workers think it isvery important to help youth nurture a sense of their cultural identity. More likely to think nurturing cultural identity is important are youth workers from congregations serving youth who are predominantly low income or African American (39 percent and 59 percent, respectively, place a very high importance on nurturing cultural identity).

When the religious community does touch youth in high-risk situations, it is generally seen as outreach or missions. Depending on the situation, the outreach can create friction if the "at-risk youth" start being assimilated with a core youth group. Issues of racism and classism become critical to address.

Part of the problem may be that many of the most successful youth work strategies (particularly among evangelical Christians) have relied on a "trickle-down" model of youth work: draw in the leaders and expect everyone else to follow. In surveying the history of youth work in the evangelical world, for example, Mark H. Senter III notes:

> *Despite the multiplied attempts to reach a generation of young people for Jesus Christ, the national/international models [for youth ministry] all targeted the same 15 to 20 percent of the youthful population—a group either described as student leaders or sharing the aspirations of such leaders. . . . The net result has produced a variety of effective ministries within a consistent strata of the high school society.*[137]

LACK OF COMMUNITY CONNECTIONS

Finally, while religious youth workers are sometimes recognized leaders in their communities, at other times they are isolated from the broader sphere of youth development work. In some cases, they only affiliate with other youth workers from their denomination and do not even know youth workers of other faiths—much less the community-based youth workers.

Reasons for the lack of connections may be many:

- Volunteer youth workers can spare only enough time to provide programming for young people; it is not a priority to them to network.

- Unless they have developed a strong sense of their goals in youth development, they may not see the value in networking with community youth workers.

- Some clergy may not accept the validity of networking with other faith traditions or secular youth workers.

FIGURE 5.13

RELIGIOUS YOUTH WORKERS' PARTICIPATION IN COLLABORATIVE ACTIVITIES

This chart shows the percentage of religious youth workers who say they have participated in various types of events with each group at least once in the past year.

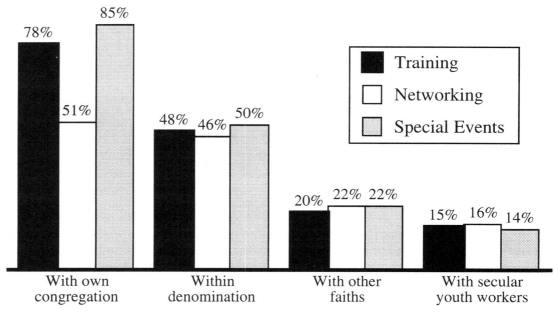

Based on Search Institute's 1995 study *The Attitudes and Needs of Religious Youth Workers: Perspectives from the Field.*

- There may be antagonism between community youth workers and religious youth workers because of different perspectives on sexuality education and other moral issues.

- Finally, they simply may not have the forums or opportunities that are conducive to developing relationships and sharing information and resources.

The 1995 survey found that only about half of religious youth workers have participated in the past year in training, networking, or special events with others from their own denomination; only a fifth have done so with other faiths, and just 15 percent have participated with secular youth workers, as Figure 5.13 displays.

We have seen both the tremendous potential and the significant barriers to integrating or enhancing a youth development emphasis into religious youth programming. In summary, several themes emerge as issues to be addressed.

LEADERSHIP

There is a clear relationship between the limited availability of accessible training and resources for volunteer and professional youth workers and the gap between goals and practice in the area of youth development. Until leadership is strengthened through training and appropriate resources, it is unlikely that positive youth development will realize its potential in religious youth organizations. As Dean writes, "Of all the gaps in Protestant, Catholic, and Jewish religious youth programs, the most threatening is the lack of accessible adult leadership training."[138]

Given this assessment, it is encouraging that 72 percent of the respondents in the 1995 survey said they wanted more training to work with youth, including 31 percent who wanted advanced training. Moreover, when asked about their participation in potential training and network-building efforts on behalf of youth, 15 percent said they would like to serve as mentors to less experienced youth workers, and 49 percent said they would be willing to serve as local leaders in organizing and maintaining such an initiative. Clearly, there is a potentially sizable leadership cadre to be mobilized in many communities.

UNDERSERVED YOUTH

While religious congregations are an almost ubiquitous presence across the country, their youth programs continue to serve primarily white, middle-class youth. And while some innovations occur, primarily at the local level, few models or resources are available to support this work, leaving a major opportunity for impact untapped. As the Carnegie report concludes: "The failure of many religious youth organizations to reach young people who face the most daunting developmental obstacles is particularly compelling in light of research indicating that religious participation and values often serve as protective factors against high-risk behaviors."[139]

An encouraging note is that the 1995 survey found that youth workers in congregations where half or more of the youth served are African American or low-income are even more interested in training and resources on the various non-sectarian youth development assets we have discussed. Substantial proportions of youth workers from these congregations—30 to 40 percent—said youth programs with a youth development focus would appeal a lot to youth who are only occasional participants or who are unconnected to congregations.

INTEGRATION

While most religious programs profess a dual emphasis on nurturing faith/cultural identity and enhancing youth development, the two emphases have, in practice, been treated as somewhat distinct and exclusive of each other. As a result, youth programs have focused their limited time and attention on the faith/cultural identity issues, neglecting youth development needs. Dean writes:

> *If spiritual growth is a matter of caring for the total person as a divine creation, then a religious youth program is inherently a multifaceted proposition. Yet religious youth programs often fail to express themselves through the full range of options available to them; developing spiritual identity often ignores the need to resolve personal struggles, and vice versa.*[140]

In reality the two goals are highly compatible and can be integrated or balanced effectively. That message is an important one to the religious community, which is already stretched in its resources and available time with youth. It suggests that learning and integrating principles of positive youth development not only addresses the goal of healthy development, but it may also more effectively nurture the faith of youth in the programs.

New models and resources are needed that bring the goals into balance. Dean puts it this way: "New models of religious youth work which hold both of these goals in balance are needed to integrate religious youth work into the entire life of the adolescent, and to integrate the adolescent into the entire life of the congregation."[141]

NETWORKING

Though a few publications and events draw youth workers together within a denomination or theological tradition, the field is largely unnetworked. Yet because of similar issues, goals, and strategies across the theological spectrum, such networks would be valuable for support and resource-sharing. "The youth programs of all religious communities possess remarkable similarities," Dean writes. "To date, however, no mechanism exists within religious communities which enable these leaders [in both Jewish and Christian traditions] to interact or dialogue about their process of outreach to youth."[142]

Furthermore, congregations need to begin cooperating with other organizations in their communities that are addressing youth issues in national, regional, and local settings. This interaction can occur at the institutional level, wherein religious youth programs coordinate programming with other nonschool youth programs.[143] In addition, opportunities for joint training and programming around issues of common concern need to be explored.

The 1995 survey of religious youth workers found that about half of youth workers would be very likely to work with other faiths in planning and sponsoring activities such as:

- assessing youth needs in the community;

- developing community service projects;

- providing youth leadership opportunities; and

- offering programs to help youth with problems they face.

Furthermore, nearly half of the religious youth workers in that survey say they would be very likely to join an interfaith network that emphasized the following activities:

- highlighting the positive role of the religious community on behalf of youth;

- making the community a better place for all youth by articulating common values and providing positive opportunities; and

- supporting each other and exchanging ideas.

In addition, new opportunities are emerging for congregations to become leading voices in communities on behalf of youth. This new openness may provide the religious community the opportunity to reclaim its public voice, advocating on behalf of young people and building bridges among competing interests in a community.

Congregations have a great opportunity to reach youth. After all, they are often the one organization in a community that young people could, if they chose, be part of. As Dean concludes in her report: "Unless religious communities undertake these challenges . . . their ability to address the needs of adolescents, spiritual or otherwise, will be severely inhibited."[144]

6.
TRANSFORMING RELIGIOUS
YOUTH WORK

We began this report with a vision for communities in which congregations actively and intentionally focus energy on building developmental strength in adolescents. We envisioned congregations as hubs of activity for the community's young people, with youth engaged as leaders and resources in their congregation and community. We imagined developmentally responsive programs in congregations in which asset building is a shared commitment.

We envisioned caring, and competent youth workers who worked across boundaries of faith traditions to find training, support, and mentoring. And, perhaps most important, we envisioned a community where more young people were growing up competent, caring, and principled because the religious community was working together (and with others) on behalf of young people.

Some elements of that vision are already in place in innovative congregations across the country. Yet we believe that, taken as a whole, this vision provides a provocative new framework and a challenge for thinking about religious youth work in the United States.

As we have surveyed the needs of adolescents, the characteristics of positive youth development, and the realities in congregational youth programs, several themes have emerged that can help shape the future of youth development efforts in congregations:

- For religious youth work to be most effective, it needs to focus and articulate its mission, then implement effective strategies for achieving that mission.

- Part of sharpening the mission and strategies involves expanding the understanding of the scope of religious youth work to include a clear commitment to nurturing healthy development, a commitment to reaching out to all types of youth, an emphasis on supporting and educating families, a congregation-wide commitment to youth, and an emphasis on community outreach and networking on behalf of youth.

- New energy needs to be placed in engaging young people meaningfully through service activities and leadership.

- Finally, religious youth workers themselves need access to training and resources to support them in their central role in congregations.

These same themes undergird Search Institute's new initiative to offer training for religious youth workers in asset building. This chapter explores these themes.

SHARPENING THE MISSION AND STRATEGIES

Like most youth work in the United States, religious youth work has relied primarily on trial-and-error approaches. Dedicated people have gathered and distilled wisdom to develop programs that address the needs they see in the young people they serve. It is often said that you don't really know anything about youth work until you have done it.

There is a large measure of truth in this approach, and it has led many creative leaders to develop innovative programs and strategies. However, too often it gives too little guidance to less creative or less experienced youth workers about where to begin, what to do, and how to approach their task.

Together with other research in areas of spiritual/faith development,[145] the emerging model of asset building provides both a framework for thinking about mission and practical strategies for setting priorities and designing programs.

Thus, asset building can help to fill an important gap in religious youth work. Search Institute's studies of both mainline Protestant congregations and a broader sample of largely Christian faith traditions show that only about half of all youth programs have a clear mission statement.[146]

Developing a shared understanding and vision for youth work is imperative in order to set priorities, make decisions, and shape programs that reinforce and build on each other. As Figure 6.1 shows, each of the characteristics of asset-building outlined in Chapter 3 have specific strategic implications for congregations.

We believe that, at its best, such a vision integrates the overlapping and integrated goals of faith/cultural nurture and positive youth development, or asset-building. It is important to note that, according to our survey of religious youth workers, non-sectarian positive youth development goals

FIGURE 6.1

CHARACTERISTICS OF EFFECTIVE ASSET-BUILDING PROGRAMS IN CONGREGATIONS (PRELIMINARY)

The following chart shows the characteristics of a congregation-based youth program based on the characteristics of effective youth development programs (see Chapter 3).*

ASSET-BUILDING THEMES	CHARACTERISTICS OF EFFECTIVE CONGREGATIONAL YOUTH PROGRAMS
Developmentally Responsive	• Programming seeks to address adolescent needs, strengths, and transitions in all areas of development. (See Figure 6.2.) • A variety of opportunities are available that respond to the interests of varied groups of adolescents; there are sufficient developmentally appropriate activities for 10, 15, and 18 year olds. • Young adolescents are permitted and encouraged to think and question. Older adolescents are trained as peer helpers to facilitate young adolescents' quest for answers. • Particular emphasis is placed on helping young people internalize and develop their personal morality, spirituality, and values.
A Positive Vision	• Leaders and members in the congregation exhibit positive attitudes toward adolescents, especially young adolescents, who are beginning to form opinions about what the congregation's adults think of them. • The youth program and the congregation have a clear mission with a stated commitment to positive youth development or asset building. • Adolescents are valued as resources and contributors in the youth program and the total congregation.
Relational Focus	• Congregations provide many opportunities for young people to form close, supportive relationships with peers, adults, and younger children, either through informal relationships or formal programs such as mentoring, peer helping, and intergenerational programs. • The congregation provides a climate where young people feel accepted, affirmed, and challenged. • Formal education programs use educational approaches (such as cooperative learning, active learning, small groups) that nurture relationship building.

This list is based on research and has not yet been tested in congregations.

FIGURE 6.1 (CONTINUED)

ASSET-BUILDING THEMES	CHARACTERISTICS OF EFFECTIVE CONGREGATIONAL YOUTH PROGRAMS
Youth Leadership	• Young people are challenged to show their competence and achievement through active participation in the congregation through leadership (in the congregation and youth program), performance (theater, music, etc.), and service. • Young people are given opportunities to express and reflect on their emerging social consciousness through service projects and other forms of activism.
Focus on the Whole Person	• In addition to their concern about spiritual development, congregations address the physical, emotional, spiritual, and intellectual needs of adolescents in their programs. • Youth development perspectives, attitudes, and approaches are infused into programming that emphasizes faith/culture nurture.
All Youth	• Youth programs do not target a specific group of youth, but seek to include a diversity of youth (ethnic, economic, etc.) in the program. • Youth programs recognize diversity as a strength. • Particular outreach efforts are made to make the program accessible and inviting to youth who are underserved by the congregation.
Cooperation Among Socializing Systems	• All primary socializing systems (families, schools, congregations) see themselves as partners in positive youth development. • Efforts are made to coordinate the messages from various socializing systems so that young people get consistent messages, particularly regarding boundaries and acceptable behavior. • The congregation enhances families in their key roles by providing education and support for parents. • The congregation encourages and supports meaningful participation by youth in their families, schools, and community organizations.
All Sectors	• Youth leaders build networks for training, support, and resource-sharing with other youth workers (denominational, other faiths, and non-sectarian) in the community. • The religious community asserts its role as a partner for youth development in the community, participating with diverse organizations in task forces, collaboratives, and other efforts on behalf of youth. • Religious youth leaders see themselves as catalysts in uniting their communities on behalf of adolescents.

are considered as important as—or even more important than—faith-specific goals for the majority of religious youth workers. Most religious youth workers see these goals as mutually supportive rather than conflicting.

EXPANDING THE BOUNDARIES OF RELIGIOUS YOUTH WORK

Another clear implication of this report is a call to broaden the understanding of religious youth work. In most traditions, a youth worker is someone who volunteers or is hired to "take care of our youth." These volunteers seek to provide a caring relationship, quality programs, and a spiritual or religious foundation for life on behalf of the congregation.

Each of those functions is important—though it is often problematic that congregations rely on one or a handful of individuals to provide those things for youth. However, expanding the boundaries of religious youth work offers new possibilities and opportunities for increasing effectiveness and impact.

HEALTHY DEVELOPMENT Just as schools are learning that it is impossible to address the educational needs of students outside the context of their emotional, physical, and other needs, congregations must do the same regarding spiritual and faith development. Current efforts to address developmental issues, when they occur, tend to be fragmented—a unit on sexuality here, a retreat on relationships there.

What's needed is to intentionally and systematically address the intellectual, physical, social, and emotional needs of youth in the context of spiritual development. This integration may influence learning activities, opportunities for social interaction, types of intellectual stimulation, and attention to young people's physical and health needs. The framework of developmental assets holds promise for developing models that address these needs.

At the same time, some of the internal assets related to self-esteem, thinking skills, and particular values may be controversial among some religious youth workers. Easing these concerns will require efforts to connect the content of these assets to theological perspectives and language that are supported by those traditions. In some cases, these youth workers may not be willing to become partners in positive youth development efforts in their community.

Search Institute's 1995 research found that there may be 20 to 30 percent of religious youth workers who have little or no interest in participating in positive youth development efforts, especially efforts that involve other faiths or secular resources. However, we also found that an equal proportion—20 to 30 percent—are very interested in *leading* such efforts!

ALL YOUTH

Religious programs for young adolescents tend to be homogeneous. While they may express openness to all youth, they typically reach only the youth whose parents participate in the congregation. Training and program materials in religious youth work have a definite focus on white, middle-class youth.

Youth leaders in most denominations and organizations recognize and are deeply concerned about this imbalance. Creative thinking and innovative approaches are needed to overcome it. And for some congregations, thinking about programs for youth "in" the congregation is largely a misnomer. In the 1995 study of religious youth workers, 11 percent of the congregations report that *half or more* of the youth they serve are not members of the congregation.

FAMILIES

Seeing parents as partners has become a major topic of conversation in religious youth work. Most program leaders recognize the central role parents play in their children's development. Indeed, a movement toward "youth and family ministry" has emerged in several Christian denominations.[147]

While innovative efforts are underway, most youth workers who participated in our 1995 survey and focus groups still struggle with how to engage parents and provide them with education and support. Thus, sharing of innovative models, effective approaches, and quality resources is needed to strengthen congregations' ability to partner with parents.

CONGREGATION-WIDE

In a fairly typical congregation, the youth program has its own coordinating committee, its own staff (volunteer and professional), and its own program. Connections to other areas of the congregation's mission are tangential or coincidental. Almost the only time the youth program is discussed by the congregation's board is when there is a problem.

Of course, there are congregations that do not fit this pattern. Particularly in some cultural and faith traditions, a strong sense of intergenerational community and shared responsibility for youth has been maintained. However, too many congregations have become as age-segregated as society at large, with youth rarely, if ever, interacting meaningfully with more than a handful of adults.

The asset-building vision calls for a new understanding that the whole community of faith has a responsibility to care for young people. Central to that vision is capitalizing on the congregation's unique opportunity to build intergenerational community. Barriers must be broken down so that youth can form caring relationships with senior citizens, their parents' peers, and young adults. In addition, they can become caring mentors and friends to younger children in the congregation.

In addition, this vision challenges congregations to evaluate many aspects of their life to determine how other activities either enhance or impede a commitment to asset building. This self-examination might include examining budget priorities, integrating youth into leadership, involving youth in worship, planning for ways all areas of congregational life can nurture assets, and much more. Only when such an examination occurs will the congregation begin to provide the kind of environment where young people are valued, connected, and nurtured by a caring community.

COMMUNITY-WIDE   What happens in neighborhoods, schools, community organizations, and other settings certainly impacts the effectiveness of congregations in building a base of developmental assets. In some communities, congregations already play a significant role as community leaders, and there already is a foundation of trust and cooperation. For example, the National Congress of Black Churches' Project SPIRIT after-school program is designed to be a unifying agent among church, family, and community.

In most cases, however, congregations are isolated from other sectors—not to mention isolated from other congregations and faith traditions. Congregations focus their energy on "our kids," and may even be antagonistic toward broad efforts in the community (particularly when issues of adolescent sexuality and pregnancy are addressed). Adding to the barriers, community-based youth workers often do not consider religious youth workers their peers.

Our 1995 data showed that only a small percentage of religious youth workers networked with secular youth workers over the previous year, and yet the important youth program goals of many secular and religious organizations are quite similar. Single institutions and sole sectors of the community cannot do it alone. Finding common ground and renewing a commitment to "public life" on behalf of adolescents is imperative to building the healthy communities in which asset building is more likely.

In addition, special efforts should be made for congregations to increase their community involvement on behalf of youth who are not connected to a religious organization. To do this, congregations could increase their commitment to family-strengthening activities, to providing collaborative after-school programs, to nurturing youth's commitment to education, and to advocate on important issues affecting youth—all of which help determine whether a community is more or less healthy for youth.

Finally, religious youth workers and clergy need to establish more relationships with appropriate secular youth-serving organizations and, especially, with broad community coalitions, to ensure that the voices of the faith communities are represented in key discussions, decisions, and initiatives regarding youth. Ideally, this participation would result in religious youth workers serving as leaders of community-wide partnerships for youth.

ENGAGING YOUTH MEANINGFULLY

Religious youth work is somewhat cyclical in its efforts to involve youth meaningfully. Believing that youth leadership is a good idea, adults turn programs over to youth, only to have them fail. So the adults take over. Eventually, they forget or think it's time again to let youth run programs. And the cycle continues. A recent study in one denomination found that only 19 percent of youth (90 percent of whom are active in their congregation) say their congregation does a "good" or "excellent" job of involving youth in decision making.[148]

If youth leadership is to be developed in and through congregations, intentional efforts will need to be made to develop skills that will increase the chances of success. Opportunities will have to be created, and risks will have to be taken.

Relatively few programs include adolescents, especially young adolescents, as active, equal participants in planning and leadership. Effective models need to be learned and shared. For example, the Center for Youth Ministry Development offers a five-day residential training program for youth called Youthleader, and the Lutheran Church-Missouri Synod project, Youth Leadership Initiative 2000, seeks to train 4,000 adolescents in leadership skills by 2001.[149]

RETHINKING YOUTH WORKER TRAINING AND SUPPORT

No less than the youth they seek to guide, religious youth workers need opportunities and supportive relationships to be most effective in their work. Yet, though religious youth workers (both professional and volunteer) are dedicated to young people, they do not have the training, networks of support, or recognition in the congregation and community that they need to work toward the vision of asset building.

What should be done to change this situation and truly tap the enormous potential of faith communities to help youth develop positively? Search Institute's experience and recent research—particularly our study of religious youth workers—offer recommendations.

GROWTH OPPORTUNITIES Whether volunteer or professional, most religious youth workers have inadequate opportunities for growth in their knowledge and understanding of adolescent development and effective youth work. While a number of training events are offered by national youth work organizations, there is clearly a need for additional options.

In our survey sample, most youth workers in congregations are volunteers, and most are part-time, whether paid or volunteer. Consideration of the demands on their time is key to the success or failure of efforts to provide training and resources. Several strategies—which will be tested in the next phase of Search Institute's work—hold promise:

- Making training available at least once per year for every youth worker, experienced or novice, paid or volunteer.

- Offering training that is both convenient and affordable. The 1995 survey suggests the ideal training would last up to one day, be offered either in January-February or July-August, and cost no more than about $50 per person.

- Offering training in local communities, rather than at a national or large regional event. Such an approach not only reduces costs, but also has the potential for stronger follow-up, networking, and impact in the local community.

- Developing training that is appropriate across faith traditions—all of which express interest in and commitment to the youth development themes. Such an approach will require a non-sectarian approach that can be supplemented by denominational or faith tradition teachings within congregations or denominations.

- Focusing training on specific program implications of the asset-building framework. This focus helps to avoid the trap of a smorgasbord of disconnected options that are difficult to evaluate or piece together into a comprehensive, integrated program. In addition, this focus complements the array of existing training opportunities that focus largely on faith development issues. Figure 5.8 highlights themes about which most youth workers expressed interest in training and resources.

- In addition to the general themes that have broad appeal, several themes have particular interest to key groups. Our survey found that potential local leaders, people with experience in secular collaboration, full-time volunteers, and those whose youth groups are mostly African American or low income are more interested than other youth workers in training and resources in the following areas: youth leadership skills; linking with other youth programs;

increasing congregations' commitment to youth; and increasing congregations' community involvement.

- Offering advanced training to seasoned youth workers. About 31 percent of our survey respondents want advanced training. Informal conversations with long-time youth work professionals suggest a similar need, as they find most youth work training to be too elementary for their needs.

- Finding ways to tap the experiences and wisdom of veteran youth workers (in addition to offering advanced training). Opportunities to be trained as trainers or becoming mentors to less-experienced colleagues offer new challenges to keep from losing energy for youth work.

Of course, this type of training will not appeal to all youth workers. We might expect indifference or disinterest by 20 percent to 30 percent of youth workers in some communities. Again, however, time, the financial cost of trainings and resources, and scheduling conflicts appear to be greater concerns.

It is conceivable that a small minority of religious youth workers may find the emphasis on non-sectarian positive youth development so much of an anathema that they would feel compelled to challenge or obstruct the efforts in communities. However, the significant interest we have seen expressed by the majority of religious youth workers in this approach suggests to us that most youth workers would not welcome such an attempt to keep them from participating.

Despite the barriers, nearly half of the religious youth workers in our survey want to *lead* the organizing and maintaining of a community initiative to provide these kinds of positive youth development trainings and resources. This level of interest bodes well for careful, responsive efforts to provide quality training in communities.

RELATIONSHIPS

In addition to the need for quality training, there is as great a need for building relationships among youth workers in communities. Most youth workers are relatively isolated from their peers in other congregations—not to mention their isolation from those working in non-sectarian agencies. It is illustrative that, in focus groups in communities, the youth workers we interviewed rarely knew each other before the conversation—even though their congregations are, in some cases, separated by only a few blocks. Thus, youth workers miss out on important opportunities for peer support, idea-swapping, and shared training and resources.

Therefore, an important component of offering effective training in communities is also to nurture an interfaith network of youth workers who can provide mutual support for each other and develop a shared vision for youth throughout the faith community. Our 1995 survey suggests that 15 percent of youth workers want to serve as mentors, and 27 percent want to have a mentor. Such a network can also allow for resource and idea-sharing between veteran and novice youth workers.

Although just 34 percent of religious youth workers are very interested in general in joining an interfaith network, more than half are very interested in specific activities, and another 39 percent are unsure whether they would join. That uncertainty suggests an openness by these youth workers to being convinced that a well-functioning local interfaith network has something to offer them.

A CHALLENGE

The vision we have described and the recommendations we've listed are not meant only to increase religious youth workers' effectiveness in working with youth. They are meant as well to build upon the relatively untapped potential of the religious community to strengthen youth work by bringing youth workers together to deal with common interests and issues across congregations and faith traditions. They are meant, ultimately, to help the religious community assert its concern for the well-being of all youth and its authority in helping set the agenda for the community's youth.

Some congregations and some youth workers will be more comfortable with the more limited goal of increasing their effectiveness in working with adolescents. But our research suggests that a majority will be open to taking up this broader challenge, and a substantial proportion will want to be leaders in that mission. It remains for that commitment to positive youth development to be tapped and focused, and for youth, youth workers, congregations, and communities to be transformed as a result.

7.
NOTES

[1] Carnegie Council on Adolescent Development, A *Matter of Time: Risk and Opportunity in the Nonschool Hours* (New York, NY: Carnegie Corporation of New York), p. 52.

[2] *Ibid.*

[3] "Remarks by the President on Religious Liberty in America at James Madison High School, Vienna, Virginia," news release from the Office of the Press Secretary, the White House (July 12, 1995).

[4] The Center for Early Adolescence, which was part of the University of North Carolina at Chapel Hill, closed in July 1995. Its resources, training, and services have been integrated into the work of Search Institute.

[5] See, for example, Eugene C. Roehlkepartain, *The Teaching Church* (Nashville, TN: Abingdon Press, 1993).

[6] Kenda Creasy Dean, *A Synthesis of the Research on, and a Descriptive Overview of Protestant, Catholic, and Jewish Religious Youth Programs in the United States* (New York, NY: Carnegie Council on Adolescent Development, 1991), p. 10.

[7] Peter C. Scales et al., *The Attitudes and Needs of Religious Youth Workers: Perspectives from the Field* (Minneapolis, MN: Search Institute, 1995).

[8] Joseph F. Kett, "Discovery and Invention in the History of Adolescence," *Journal of Adolescent Health* (1993), Vol. 14, pp. 605-612.

[9] Carnegie Council on Adolescent Development, p. 9.

[10] Peter C. Scales, *A Portrait of Young Adolescents in the 1990s* (Carrboro, NC: The Center for Early Adolescence, 1991), p. 8.

[11] An interesting example of the chasm between the general field of youth development and religious youth work is that it is rare for a secular resource on young adolescent development to even mention spiritual or moral development—except, perhaps, in the context of intellectual development.

[12] John H. Westerhoff III, *Will Our Children Have Faith?* (Minneapolis, MN: Winston Press, 1980), p. 26.

[13] Peter L. Benson, *The Troubled Journey: A Portrait of 6th-12th Grade Youth* (Minneapolis, MN: Search Institute, 1990), p. 44.

[14] *The Troubled Journey* defines binge drinking as having five or more drinks in a row, once or more in the past two weeks. Frequent use of illicit drugs is defined as having used marijuana, cocaine or crack, PCP, LSD, amphetamines, heroin, or other narcotics six or more times in the past 12 months. Sexual activity is defined as having sexual intercourse two or more times in lifetime. Vandalism is defined as destroying property "just for fun" two or more times in the past 12 months.

[15] Carnegie Council on Adolescent Development, p. 27. Also see *Beyond Rhetoric: A New American Agenda for Children and Families* (Washington, DC: National Commission on Children, 1991), p. 53.

[16] Peter C. Scales and C. Kenneth McEwin, *Growing Pains: The Making of America's Middle School Teachers* (Carrboro, NC: The Center for Early Adolescence and Columbus, OH: National Middle School Association, 1994).

[17] The only magazine designed for leaders of this age group in religious settings is titled *Jr. High Ministry.* (published by Group Publishing, Loveland, CO). The best-known book on the subject among evangelicals is Wayne Rice, *Junior High Ministry.* For a Roman Catholic perspective, see John Roberto, editor, *Access Guides to Youth Ministry: Early Adolescent Ministry* (New Rochelle, NY: Don Bosco Multimedia, 1991).

[18] Carnegie Council on Adolescent Development, pp. 28-35.

[19] "After School," *Education Week* (May 3, 1995), p. 4.

[20] Cited in Scales, *A Portrait of Young Adolescents in the 1990s*, p. 43.

[21] Laurence Steinberg and Ann Levine, *You and Your Adolescent: A Parent's Guide for Ages 10-20* (Harper & Row, 1990), pp. 1, 3.

[22] Joan Wynn et al., *Communities and Adolescents: A Exploration of Reciprocal Supports* (New York: Youth and America's Future: The William T. Grant Foundation Commission on Work, Family and Citizenship, 1988).

[23] *Speaking of Kids: A National Study of Children and Parents* (Washington, DC: National Commission on Children, 1991), p. 13.

[24] Benson, *The Troubled Journey*, p. 11.

[25] Peter L. Benson and Carolyn H. Eklin, *Effective Christian Education: A National Study of Protestant Congregations—A Summary Report on Faith, Loyalty, and Congregational Life* (Minneapolis, MN: Search Institute, 1990), p. 48.

[26] David Elkind, *The Hurried Child* (Reading, MA: Addison-Wesley, 1981), and *All Grown Up and No Place to Go* (Reading, MA: Addison-Wesley, 1984).

[27] Elkind, *The Hurried Child*, p. 118.

[28] Elkind, *All Grown Up and No Place to Go*, p. 94.

[29] See, especially, Wellesley College Center for Research on Women, *How Schools Shortchange Girls* (Washington, DC: AAUW Educational Foundation, 1992).

[30] Jacquelynne S. Eccles et al., "Development During Adolescence: The Importance of Stage-Environment Fit on Young Adolescents' Experiences in Schools and in Families," *American Psychologist*, 48 (2), pp. 90-101.

[31] Cited in Scales, *A Portrait of Young Adolescents in the 1990s*, p. 21.

[32] "Cities Record Record Numbers of Killings, Youths Play Grim Role," *New York Times* (January 1, 1994), p. 7A.

[33] Scales, *A Portrait of Young Adolescents in the 1990s*, p. 8.

[34] Karen J. Pittman and Michelle Cahill, *A New Vision: Promoting Youth Development* (Washington, DC: Center for Youth Development and Policy Research, 1991), p. 3.

[35] In *A Matter of Time*, the Carnegie Council on Adolescent Development defines positive youth development as **"the process through which adolescents actively seek, and are assisted, to meet their basic needs and build their individual assets or competencies."**

Three other resources are relevant: Karen J. Pittman, *A Rationale for Enhancing the Role of the Non-School Voluntary Sector in Youth Development* (Washington, DC: Center for Youth Development and Policy Research, Academy for Educational Development, 1991); Karen J. Pittman and Michelle Cahill, *A New Vision: Promoting Youth Development*; and *Building Resiliency: What Works!* (Washington, DC: The National Assembly, 1994).

[36] Benson, *The Troubled Journey*, p. 7.

[37] Peter L. Benson, *Uniting Communities for Youth* (Minneapolis, MN: Search Institute, 1995), p. 6.

[38] *Ibid.*, pp. 9-10.

[39] Karen J. Pittman identified a compatible list of five areas of "competence" that can also be considered important internal assets:

- Health/physical competence
- Personal/social competence
- Cognitive/creative competence
- Vocational competence
- Citizenship competence (ethics and participation).

See Pittman, *A Rationale for Enhancing the Role of the Non-School Voluntary Sector in Youth Development*, pp. 15-16.

[40] Additional assets are being identified, and the list will be expanded after further research.

[41] *Building Resiliency*, pp. 30-32.

[42] Steinberg and Levine, p. 2.

[43] *Building Resiliency*, p. 38.

[44] Cited in Scales, *A Portrait of Young Adolescents in the 1990s*, p. 9.

[45] *Building Resiliency*, p. 28.

[46] Benson, *Uniting Communities for Youth*, p. 12.

[47]T. Ooms and L. Herendeen, *Integrated Approaches to Youths' Health Problems: Federal, State, and Community Roles* (Washington, DC: Family Impact Seminar, American Association for Marriage and Family Therapy, 1989).

[48]Carnegie Council on Adolescent Development, p. 21.

[49]*Building Resiliency,* p. 34.

[50]Peter C. Scales, *Connecting Schools and Middle Schools: Strategies for Preparing Middle-Level Teachers* (Carrboro, NC: Center for Early Adolescence, 1995), p. 16.

[51]"Churches Rated Best Able to Deal with Local Community Problems," *PRRC Emerging Trends* (December, 1990), p. 3.

[52]Indeed, virtually all of the "prevention" programs that are currently considered effective have as a foundation the *promotion* of self-competencies and other assets. See, for example, Todd Rogers, Beth Howard-Pitney, and Bonnie L. Bruce, *What Works? A Guide to School-Based Alcohol and Drug Abuse Prevention Curricula* (Palo Alto, CA: Health Promotion Resource Center, Stanford Center for Research in Disease Prevention, 1989).

[53]Benson, *Uniting Communities for Youth,* p. 10.

[54]Cited in Carnegie Council on Adolescent Development, p. 37.

[55]*Ibid.,* p. 35.

[56]Benson, *Uniting Communities for Youth,* p. 10.

[57]Pittman, *A Rationale for Enhancing the Role of the Non-School Voluntary Sector in Youth Development,* p. 48.

[58]Benson, *The Troubled Journey,* p. 78.

[59]Scales et al., *The Attitudes and Needs of Religious Youth Workers.*

[60]Roberta G. Simmons and Dale A. Blyth, *Moving into Adolescence: The Impact of Pubertal Change and School Context* (New York, NY: Aldine de Gruyter, 1987).

[61]Dean, p. 45.

[62]Because of the heavy focus on faith nurture and religious identity (which are beyond the scope of this project), this paper will focus most heavily on the youth groups—the informal education—not formal religious education. However, the formal education settings can also be enriched by an understanding of youth development, just as public education is enhanced by this emphasis.

[63]For the purposes of this paper, worship will only be addressed as it relates to opportunities for enhancing youth development, not for its central purpose in the sacramental or devotional life of the faith community.

[64]Dean, p. 47.

[65]*Ibid.,* p. 50.

[66]Roehlkepartain, *The Teaching Church,* p. 76.

[67]*Ibid.,* p. 75.

[68]*Ibid.,* p. 81.

[69]Dean, pp. 75-76.

[70]Eugene C. Roehlkepartain (editor), *The Youth Ministry Resource Book* (Loveland, CO: Group Books, 1987), p. 184.

[71]See, for example, Benson, *The Troubled Journey,* p. 13.

[72]Dean, p. 60.

[73]Robert Bezilla, editor, *America's Youth in the 1990s* (Princeton, NJ: George H. Gallup International Institute, 1993), p. 153.

[74]Benson and Eklin, p. 50.

[75]Carnegie Council on Adolescent Development, p. 53.

[76]Dean, p. 33.

[77]*Ibid.,* pp. 33-34.

[78]Based on data first reported in Benson and Eklin. Sample includes youth from the Christian Church (Disciples of Christ); Evangelical Church in America; Presbyterian Church (USA), United Methodist Church; and United Church of Christ.

[79] Based on Search Institute research for Project Affirmation, a study for the Boards of Education, North American Division of the Seventh-Day Adventist Church, 1990-1991.

[80] Peter L. Benson, Eugene C. Roehlkepartain, and I. Shelby Andress, *Congregations at Crossroads: A National Portrait of Adults and Youth in The Lutheran Church–Missouri Synod* (Minneapolis, MN: Search Institute, 1995).

[81] Dean notes that participation in Jewish supplementary schools decreased by 52 percent between 1962 and 1986, while Jewish day schools doubled in size. Also see Sylvia Barack Fishman and Alice Goldstein, *When They Are Grown They Will Not Depart: Jewish Education and the Jewish Behavior of Adults* (Waltham, MA: Cohen Center for Modern Jewish Studies at Brandeis University, 1993), pp. 1-3.

[82] Mark H. Senter III, "Trickle-Down Strategies Come to an End: The Youth Ministry Revolution," *Youthworker Journal* (Summer 1994), pp. 38-44. Senter notes particularly that Youth for Christ is currently experiencing serious financial problems. Other programs are also re-evaluating their approaches to youth work.

[83] "High involvement" is defined as attending religious services at least once or twice a month. "Low involvement" is defined as rarely or never attending religious services.

[84] Binge drinking is defined as having five or more drinks in a row, once or more in the past two weeks. Problem drug use is defined as having used marijuana, cocaine or crack, PCP, LSD, amphetamines, heroin, or other narcotics six or more times in the past 12 months. Sexual activity is defined as having sexual intercourse two or more times in lifetime. Attempted suicide is defined as having attempted suicide once or more in lifetime.

[85] Carolyn H. Eklin and Eugene C. Roehlkepartain, "The Faith Factor: What Role Can Churches Play in At-Risk Prevention?" *Source* (Search Institute quarterly newsletter), pp. 1-3. Also see Bernard Spilka, Ralph W. Hood, Jr., and Richard L. Gorsuch, *The Psychology of Religion: An Empirical Approach* (Englewood Cliffs, NJ: Prentice Hall, 1985); and Dean, pp. 22-26.

[86] Eugene C. Roehlkepartain and Peter L. Benson, *Youth in Protestant Churches* (Minneapolis, MN: Search Institute, 1993), p. 99. In this study, highly active youth are those who say they attend worship services weekly AND participate in other activities six hours or more per month AND spend six or more hours doing volunteer work at their congregation each month.

[87] Roger L. Dudley with V. Bailey Gillespie, *Valuegenesis: Faith in the Balance* (Riverside, CA: La Sierra University Press, 1992), p. 263.

[88] Dudley, p. 266.

[89] Quoted in Dean, p. 27.

[90] *Ibid.*, p. 27.

[91] Peter L. Benson, *Religion, Religious Institutions, and the Development of Caring,* presentation to the Lilly Endowment Conference on Youth and Caring, Key Biscayne, Florida, February 26-27, 1992.

[92] Erickson, p. 109.

[93] Cited in Carnegie Council on Adolescent Development, p 52.

[94] Dean, p. 38.

[95] Dean R. Hoge et al., "Desired Outcomes of Religious Education and Youth Ministry in Six Denominations" *Review of Religious Research*, (23), pp. 230-254.

[96] Roehlkepartain, *The Teaching Church*, pp. 76-77.

[97] Dean, pp. 42-44.

[98] Greek Orthodox Archdiocese Teenage Task Force on Religious Education, *The Church at Risk: Meeting the Challenging Needs of Teenagers Today* (Brookline, MA: Greek Orthodox Archdiocese of North and South America, 1988), p. 2.

[99] *A Vision of Youth Ministry* (Washington, DC: Department of Education, United States Catholic Conference, 1986), p. 7.

[100] "Youth Ministry Objectives" from the Southern Baptist Sunday School Board, n.d.

[101] For example, the Assemblies of God's mission statement is "to win, build, and send youth." None of the five objectives mentions healthy development. The *Aaronic Priesthood Leadership Handbook* from the Young Men Organization of the Church of Jesus Christ of Latter-Day Saints does not include any references to

healthy development, though the LDS commitment to healthy development is well-known.

102"Church Membership Continues to Rise," *PRRC Emerging Trends* (April, 1993), p. 5.

103"Church Attendance Remarkably Constant," *PRRC Emerging Trends* (March, 1993), p. 5.

104"Life Cycle Changes Are Leading to More Frequent Church Attendance," *PRRC Emerging Trends* (June, 1991), p. 2.

105George Gallup Jr., editor, *The Unchurched American: Ten Years Later* (Princeton, NJ: Princeton Religious Research Center, 1988), p. 61.

106Roehlkepartain and Benson, *Youth in Protestant Churches*, p. 65.

107*Ibid.*, p. 129.

108Virginia A. Hodgkinson and Murray S. Weitzman, *Volunteering and Giving Among American Teenagers 12 to 17 Years of Age: Findings From a National Survey* (Washington, DC: Independent Sector, 1992), p. 38.

109"Churches' Role in Social Change Eyed by Researchers," *National Christian Reporter* (February 5, 1993).

110"The Children We Have in Trust," *Sojourners* (April, 1994), pp. 14-18.

111*Ibid.*, pp. 111-113.

112Roehlkepartain and Benson, *Youth in Protestant Churches*, Chapter 4.

113See Scales, *A Portrait of Young Adolescents in the 1990s*, p. 36-41.

114Dean, pp. 77-78.

115*Ibid.*, p. 77.

116*Ibid.*, p. 83. The two are the Center for Youth Ministry Development's "Early Adolescent Ministry Institute," and Group Publishing's "Youth Ministry Consultant" certification program for junior high ministry.

117*Ibid.*, p. 80.

118*Ibid.*, p. 87.

119*Ibid.*, p. 85.

120Barack Fishman and Goldstein, p. 2.

121Dean, pp. 79-80.

122*Ibid.*, p. 43.

123For example, considerable controversy has surrounded the use of the Lions-Quest youth development curriculum, *Skills for Adolescence,* in both private and public schools. Criticisms of the curriculum include the following: "Lions-Quest's core philosophy, its goals, and its techniques are humanistic, and, therefore, should be rejected out of hand. . . . Self-esteem is a product of humanism. It is man-centered rather than Christ-centered. . . . Support of the program, even if lukewarm, supports a philosophy diametrically opposed to Christianity. . . . Lions-Quest contributes to the cumulative effects of humanistic permissiveness in areas such as abortion, pornography, sexual perversion, drug use, and human abuse." Quoted in *Questioning Quest: The Use of Lions-Quest Materials in Lutheran Schools* (Minneapolis, MN: Lutheran Brotherhood, n.d.), pp. 4-5.

124While we found broad interest in interfaith cooperation in general, some religious groups are unlikely to cooperate with certain other groups for theological reasons. More than half of respondents say they are willing to work with mainline Protestants (72 percent), Catholic (65 percent), and evangelical Christian (62 percent). But fewer than half say they are willing to work with Jews (45 percent), charismatic or Pentecostal Christians (39 percent), fundamentalist Christians (37 percent), Muslims (21 percent), or Mormons (16 percent). These findings suggest that people's definitions of "interfaith" vary considerably, and significant work would be involved in building trust and respect across all these faith traditions.

125Search Institute's *Effective Christian Education* study found that only 27 percent of mainline Protestant congregations emphasize education about sexuality, and 20 percent emphasize education about alcohol and other drugs.

126See, for example, G. Keith Olson, *Counseling Teenagers* (Loveland, CO: Group Books, 1984).

127For example, *Youthworker Journal* asked 21 leaders in evangelical youth ministry to speculate on the future of youth work in the year 2010. Many of these leaders focused on "dysfunctional families" and other problems. Only three addressed themes of positive youth development. See "Where Are We Headed: Christian Leaders Speak Out About the Future of Youth Ministry," *Youthworker Journal* (Summer, 1994), pp. 30-37.

[128] See Roehlkepartain, *The Teaching Church*, and Benson and Eklin.

[129] Jolene L. Roehlkepartain, "Jr. High Ministry Comes of Age," *Jr. High Ministry Magazine* (January/February, 1988), pp. 4-10.

[130] Roehlkepartain, *The Teaching Church*, p. 177.

[131] Benson, Roehlkepartain, and Andress, *Congregations at Crossroads*, p. 22.

[132] Dean, p. 69.

[133] The CNBC sponsors a variety of programs aimed particularly at addressing the needs of at-risk youth. These include: Project SPIRIT, a church-based after-school program; and the National Anti-Drug Campaign, which seeks "to leverage the influence of the black church and its clergy in mobilizing communities to combat the epidemic of drug abuse and its associated crime." See "The Congress of National Black Churches" informational brochure.

[134] Dean reports that Youth for Christ is the only parachurch group that "named service to at-risk teenagers as a signature feature of its work" (p. 69).

[135] See, for example, Eugene C. Roehlkepartain, *Youth Ministry in City Churches* (Loveland, CO: Group Books, 1989).

[136] Quoted in Roehlkepartain, *Youth Ministry in City Churches*, p. 115. This book was written specifically to provide a foundational resource on urban religious youth work. However, it is no longer in print (though still distributed by Search Institute), and no other resources are currently available.

[137] Senter, pp. 38-44.

[138] Dean, p. 102.

[139] Carnegie Council on Adolescent Development, p. 54.

[140] Dean, p. 114.

[141] *Ibid.*, p. 114.

[142] *Ibid.*, p. 117.

[143] *Ibid.*, p. 119.

[144] *Ibid.*, p. 123.

[145] See, for example, Roehlkepartain, *The Teaching Church*.

[146] *Ibid.*, p. 97.

[147] A leading voice in this movement is the Augsburg Youth and Family Institute at Augsburg College, Minneapolis, Minnesota, which has developed a comprehensive model and supporting materials for youth and family ministry.

[148] Benson, Roehlkepartain, and Andress, p. 23.

[149] One popular resource and model is found in Thom and Joani Schultz, *Kids Taking Charge: Youth-Led Youth Ministry* (Loveland, CO: Group Publishing, 1987).